CW00516169

The **SCHOOL** of **WELLBEING**

by the same author

How to Create Kind Schools
12 extraordinary projects making schools
happier and helping every child fit in
Jenny Hulme
Foreword by Claude Knights, CEO of Kidscape
ISBN 978 1 84905 591 8
eISBN 978 1 78450 157 0

of related interest

Using Poetry to Promote Talking and Healing
Pooky Knightsmith
ISBN 978 1 78592 053 0
eISBN 978 1 78450 323 9

Self-Harm and Eating Disorders in Schools
A Guide to Whole-School Strategies and Practical Support
Pooky Knightsmith
ISBN 978 1 84905 584 0
eISBN 978 1 78450 031 3

LEGO®-Based Therapy
How to build social competence through LEGO®-based
Clubs for children with autism and related conditions
ISBN 978 1 84905 537 6
eISBN 978 0 85700 960 9

Starving the Exam Stress Gremlin
A Cognitive Behavioural Therapy Workbook on
Managing Exam Stress for Young People
Kate Collins-Donnelly
Part of the *Gremlin and Thief CBT Workbooks* series
ISBN 978 1 84905 698 4
eISBN 978 1 78450 214 0

That's So Gay!
Challenging Homophobic Bullying
Jonathan Charlesworth
ISBN 978 1 84905 461 4
eISBN 978 0 85700 837 4

The SCHOOL of WELLBEING

12 Extraordinary Projects
Promoting Children and Young People's
Mental Health and Happiness

JENNY HULME

Jessica Kingsley *Publishers*
London and Philadelphia

First published in 2017
by Jessica Kingsley Publishers
73 Collier Street
London N1 9BE, UK
and
400 Market Street, Suite 400
Philadelphia, PA 19106, USA

www.jkp.com

Copyright © Jenny Hulme 2017

Front cover image source: iStockphoto®.

All rights reserved. No part of this publication may be reproduced in any
material form (including photocopying, storing in any medium by electronic
means or transmitting) without the written permission of the copyright owner
except in accordance with the provisions of the law or under terms of a licence
issued in the UK by the Copyright Licensing Agency Ltd. www.cla.co.uk or in
overseas territories by the relevant reproduction rights organisation, for details
see www.ifrro.org. Applications for the copyright owner's written permission to
reproduce any part of this publication should be addressed to the publisher.

Warning: The doing of an unauthorised act in relation to a copyright work may
result in both a civil claim for damages and criminal prosecution.

Library of Congress Cataloging in Publication Data
Names: Hulme, Jenny, author.
Title: The school of wellbeing : 12 extraordinary projects promoting children and
young people's mental health and happiness / Jenny Hulme.
Other titles: School of well-being
Description: London : Jessica Kingsley Publishers, 2017. | Includes index.
Identifiers: LCCN 2016038901 | ISBN 9781785920967 (alk. paper)
Subjects: LCSH: Students--Mental health. | School mental health services.
| Well-being.
Classification: LCC LB3430 .H85 2017 | DDC 371.7/13--dc23 LC record
available at https://lccn.loc.gov/2016038901

British Library Cataloguing in Publication Data
A CIP catalogue record for this book is available from the British Library

ISBN 978 1 78592 096 7
eISBN 978 1 78450 359 8

Printed and bound in Great Britain

Acknowledgements

With huge thanks to everyone who shared their experience and expertise with me while I was writing these stories. Your commitment to a better, healthier and happier education system (and the wellbeing of every single child) completely inspired me. Also to Mark Blayney for his invaluable advice, to my editors at Jessica Kingsley Publishers for getting behind this book and to my children, Scott and Eleni, for helping me to write it.

Contents

Introduction

We're in a packed theatre, giving a spontaneous standing ovation to Ruby Wax at the end of her show *Frazzled*. There's nothing like being part of a crowd like this to remind us that there is, finally, a new way of thinking about mental health. Dubbed the poster girl of the subject (and she's picked up an OBE for services to it), the actor and author wryly confesses at the start of her one-woman show that she's made a new career out of her experience of depression, before candidly and comically sharing her exploration of it.

During the closing part of the event Wax invites the audience into the debate and a student stands up and asks her what she thinks can be done about the problems in schools; in particular the pressures on students and the mental health problems they exacerbate. When Wax asks the audience if there is anyone who *doesn't* recognise the problem we're seeing in education and believes there is no need for change, no one in the 3000 plus crowd raises their hand.

Many, though, might be left wondering why the student in question felt compelled to get to her feet. Why, when this subject is now the stuff of sell out shows, of magazine articles, the focus of bestselling books and even Royal patronages (at the time of writing the Duke and Duchess of Cambridge and Prince Harry are joining forces to launch the Heads Together Campaign to help destigmatise the issue), are we not seeing the real benefits in the classroom?

There can be no doubt there's an appetite for change. Consider the 39 million plus hits on TED when Sir Ken Robinson suggested dance be given the same priority as maths, or the huge number of YouTube viewings of Sir Anthony Seldon talking about the role of education in building happier societies. Look at the growing crowd (most teachers and many business leaders, children's charities and pupils) behind the campaign to make PSHE – the subject that most directly promotes emotional wellbeing – statutory. So why is there still sluggishness on this issue? 'Never mind university,' says Ruby Wax. 'I always wonder what institutions they think these kids will be in when they're 40?'

As slowly and surely as we're seeing the stigma around mental health being put aside, we are seeing the gaps that need to be filled in young people's education so they can build their emotional wellbeing for the future. A golden opportunity for change.

This change comes not before time. Schools – even if they haven't properly understood all the issues and the impact they have – now know that in an average classroom ten young people will have witnessed their parents separate. One will have experienced the death of a parent. Seven will have been bullied. And research suggests one in four young people in secondary school will, at some point, have been severely neglected, physically attacked or sexually abused.

Meanwhile these children have seen their families go through a recession and are themselves facing bleaker job prospects and the impact of round the clock social media, which all exacerbate existing problems, creating a perfect storm that affects them as much as it affects their parents and carers. Teachers are aware that the growing number of school refusers may simply end up at home, unable to access the support they need to get back into school. Despite this, many feel unable to do more than send a letter home reminding families about attendance. They are no longer surprised to learn that rates of depression and anxiety among teenagers have increased by 70 per cent in the past 25 years[1] and one in ten children and young people (aged 5–16) suffer from a diagnosable mental health disorder and as many as one in 15 children and young people deliberately self-harm.[2] Some 55 per cent of children who have been bullied develop depression as adults.[3] One in four young people in the UK experience suicidal thoughts and, shockingly, suicide is the second leading cause of death in 15–29-year-olds[4] (after road traffic accidents), and the biggest single killer of men under 45 in the UK.[5] Meanwhile, the charity Young Minds has talked about the number of calls they get to their helplines as a result of exam pressure.

Rather than an *en masse* shaking of heads and wringing of hands in staff rooms about the troubles children are bringing into school (as may have been the case not so long ago), schools have learned that the years when children are in their care are the years when mental health develops, and patterns are set for the future. They recognise that resilience is something schools can help their pupils develop and that it's not about ridding life of fears, anxieties and challenges, but about building something strong in

---

1   Young Minds (2016a) Mental Health Statistics. Available at www.youngminds. org.uk/training_services/policy/mental_health_statistics, accessed on 30 August 2016.
2   Young Minds (2016b) Mental Health Statistics. Available at www.youngminds. org.uk/about/whats_the_problem/mental_health_statistics, accessed on 30 August 2016.
3   Young Minds (2016b)
4   Young Mind (2016b)
5   CALM (2014) FAQ and Suicide Stats & Research. Available at www. thecalmzone.net/about-calm/faq and www.thecalmzone.net/about-calm/ suicide-research-stats, accessed on 30 August 2016.

children and teenagers so they can understand life's problems and themselves better. They know education can help do that.

So what next?

Schools know better than anyone that greater awareness and good intentions are never enough. While they may welcome the shift in thinking, and the impact it could have, not only on their pupils' health, but on their learning and future, they too often feel stymied by a lack of training, resources and support to make the difference they'd really like to make. Teachers know that while children are at school they are in a unique position to reach them but – and here's the rub – they're also coping with the day-to-day priorities and pressures of school life, including levels of competition and performance anxiety that some teachers admit are only making the problem worse. Government messages (about character education and emotional wellbeing) appear to support what schools want to do but are delivered alongside the back-to-basics education, more onerous assessments and a narrowing of the curriculum that has seen vocational and arts subjects squeezed on the timetable. It's these vocational and arts subjects that many believe promote wellbeing.

And when schools turn to their partners in healthcare for help, they face reports that the NHS is so stretched that the vulnerable young people sent their way by schools might have to wait too long – in some cases more than a year – to get any expert support. They might not even get any help at all if their mental health issues are not considered serious enough to instigate urgent intervention. Meanwhile, they hear from charities such as the NSPCC that the number of calls from children reporting loneliness, self-harm and suicidal thoughts is on the rise.

'Schools can feel subject to so many contradictory pressures that many don't know what to do,' says Katherine Weare, Emeritus

Professor at the University of Southampton and an international expert on child mental health. 'Schools know that mental health is their business. The stigma around these issues is being reduced, and there is understanding that children's wellbeing (or lack of it) impacts on how they learn. But with every new demand on the curriculum, on tests and on their time, teachers can feel tempted to believe that messages about mental health and anything good that came before – initiatives like Every Child Matters for example – have to be set aside. As a result many schools are still unhappy places and getting unhappier, feeling the weight of getting pupils through tests and exams.'

Professor Tanya Byron, broadcaster, writer and clinical psychologist who specialises in working with children and adolescents, believes it's time to give those teachers more training and support. 'Their job is to educate and empower children through learning. That's what they signed up for,' she says. 'But they don't have mandatory mental health training and while they see the problem, they can feel powerless to help.' Professor Byron believes we need to start thinking in a different way about education, and see that learning and development is holistic and built around emotional and psychological markers as well as the ability to sit down and learn and take exams.

'At the moment we have an education system obsessed with league tables, and the focus and the investment is on grades,' she says. 'They are seen as the marker of self-worth and that has got to change. We have to tackle the disconnect between education and mental health at policy level, look at how the funding is siloed and encourage more joined up thinking about prevention.'

'I think we have been batting around responsibility for this issue,' agrees Mick Atkinson, who worked as Head of Commissioning at children's mental health charity Place2Be (more on pp.77–85). He suggests that for too long this has been an issue left with the health sector, which has in turn created a culture where we're over-reliant on health services where the focus is on treating, not preventing, difficulties. 'But there are so many knock-on beneficiaries of promoting good mental health – from education to employment to the penal system,' he says. 'Policy makers miss an opportunity by not pooling resources, while individual players feel frustrated and under threat, and so can too easily close ranks. In education that can cause a continuing focus on achieving better results and "managing bad behaviour". Meanwhile healthcare continues to focus on treating adults when problems become acute, and prisons on building bigger prisons, and so the cycle goes on. When you're in the middle of it it's hard to see how you can step out of the box and change things. Schools who do it demonstrate bravery and strong leadership.'

The Young People's Mental Health Coalition, of which Mick Atkinson is the Chair of Schools and Colleges Workstream, has four policy asks: new training for teachers, so they can better understand children's emotional and mental health, including more support and CPD (continued professional development) once they're in post; better mental health support when it's needed; a system that finds a better balance between wellbeing and attainment, and schools which are better connected to both families and social care.

'We are talking in terms of entitlement,' says Atkinson. 'If you have a broken leg or chronic asthma you are entitled to support. But the same rule doesn't seem to apply if you have emerging mental health problems.

'These issues are often seen as behavioural ones,' he adds. 'Schools are really good at picking up problems with behaviour, but it seems they don't always have the skills, services or budget to respond with the right early interventions.'

'We are, I hope, seeing that the old-fashioned view of behaviour as something children have totally under control, something they do on purpose to disrupt the class, does not always reflect reality,' adds Professor Weare. 'Difficult behaviour is not always something that can be sorted out by sanctions and better classroom management. Children don't always kick off, and they certainly don't engage in self-harm to be annoying, but because they have an emotional need.' She suggests we're now seeing schools getting underneath the word 'behaviour', understanding how the mind and brain work and realising that children's actions have complex origins. 'Schools are realising that children simply can't learn effectively if they have unmet emotional needs, such as feeling safe and secure.'

So what can your school do?

Professor Weare's paper on emotional wellbeing and her 'whole school' approach sets out a vision of a school where mental health and emotional wellbeing is everyone's business (and starts with greater care and support for the school staff). It's a vision where the culture of the school makes it acceptable to acknowledge difficulties, and to ask for help. The climate, she asserts, should be one of connectedness, a feeling of being accepted, respected and bonded to the school environment. Interventions should be rapid in their response, and involve parents and carers too.

The best solutions and most effective interventions aren't necessarily complicated, adds Mick Atkinson. 'I think teachers can sometimes feel scared and slightly overwhelmed at having to take this on; but we need to stress it isn't about treating mental illness, but about promoting mental health and emotional wellbeing in the same way as we promote physical health. Children have a right to have these things acknowledged and prioritised.'

Mick Atkinson's charity, Place2Be (more of which on pp.77–85) is proving how powerful that can be; but his message, and that of other contributors featured in this book, is to simply start somewhere. That can be with better PSHE lessons or lunchtime clubs, anti-bullying initiatives or a social action programme, mindfulness training or a mentoring programme. These and other ideas are all explored in the following pages and each illustrates that when mental health is made to matter, those initial ideas and interventions often work their way into a school culture. They seem to empower teachers to see that this – what they have always known is as important as maths and English – can be combined to support learning in those subjects. What's more, rather than feeling thwarted by their lack of time and training, the same initiatives reveal the wealth of expertise and resources already available to them: via the pupils in their own schools, the staff patrolling the playground, the companies around them, which have a vested interest in a local workforce, and the charities and organisations who can bring a wealth of expertise right into the school where and when it's needed most.

Crucially, the ideas explored in these pages can open up the whole school to possibilities and trigger other significant initiatives. They can extend magnificently outwards into the corridors and classrooms, making children's happiness and security as high a priority as any SATs tests. It speaks volumes for the work being done that this book could have been filled several times over with stories of wonderful schools that have made a difference. The 12 that follow serve to illustrate that when you start making mental health matter more, things do slowly and surely start to change.

The Children and Young People's Mental Health Coalition brings together leading charities to campaign jointly on the mental health and wellbeing of children and young people. In their section for schools you can read some case histories about schools promoting mental health and download their report on resilience and results and a document outlining a whole school and college approach to young people's mental health and emotional wellbeing. Visit www.cypmhc.org.uk/schools.

Professor Katherine Weare has developed new guidance for schools (*What works in promoting social and emotional well-being and responding to mental health problems in schools?*) for **The National Children's Bureau**. This charity has been working for over 50 years to champion the rights or children and young people and to reduce the impact on inequalities. They know education is a powerful force in transforming the lives of young people and have a whole number of initiatives, projects and partnerships to support work in schools. Visit www.ncb.org.uk to find out more.

1

The Mentor

Unlocking Your School's Powerful Resource to Build Resilience

Most pupils in a classroom will, if asked, say they know it's right to care for other people. Mentoring gives them the opportunity to prove it, and to learn more about themselves as they do. We visited two secondary schools to see what they discovered when peer mentors got to work.

'As children go through high school, being valued by a peer group can feel as important as being part of a family – more important sometimes. If a student's unhappy it's usually because they are isolated and lonely…'

KIRSTY CUNNINGHAM, ASSISTANT HEAD
TEACHER, NESTON HIGH SCHOOL

The most difficult thing about school for Maisie is the start of the day, and almost as hard are the breaks and lunchtimes. As soon as she arrives in the morning her stomach seems to clench. It's not that she doesn't want to go to school, she says, but she hates walking in on her own – seeing others in her class with their arms linked and heads together talking about what they did the day before or making plans for the weekend. She hates walking through groups of teenagers (she's in year 8 and 12 years old) who, it seems, don't even notice her as they crowd into the school. And she hates the fact that she is already being put into the bottom set when she knows she hasn't shown the school her best. None of this is seen by the teachers, or voiced by Maisie. 'There's a new girl in the class and I am really hoping I might make friends with her,' she says. 'I like the other girls, I just haven't got into one of their groups so I am often on my own.'

In another secondary school 30 miles across the county border, 12-year-old Ryan knows what Maisie is feeling, but also knows a guy called Martin has his back. Ryan is one of 40 pupils in his year being mentored. Every morning his year 10 buddy looks out for him and they do 15 minutes of reading or maths together before class starts. Later, they might arrange to meet during break time or lunchtime for a chat if Ryan hasn't got anyone to hang out with. 'He's more like a big brother than a best friend, but it's great having him around to talk to,' says Ryan. 'And he's helped me get into a chess club at school where I've got to know other boys in my year. Some weeks now I am so busy with my mates I only meet Martin in the morning, but I know he's there for me. If he sees me at the bus stop he'll come and hang out and sit by me on the way home.'

It's these simple things – having a friendly face to welcome you when you arrive at school, someone to turn to if you are finding something difficult, and a mate looking out for you on what can seem like the battle zone of the school field – which can often be overlooked by adults (or feel like something out of their control). But in schools around the UK, hard-pressed teachers are starting to see that the one resource they are missing in their desire to support students who struggle is students themselves. Every mentoring scheme seems to suggest that there are scores of young people ready to rise to the challenge of helping their peers build confidence and resilience as they navigate their way through school. They're not only proving the most powerful of learning tools, but also one of the first lines of defence against loneliness and social anxiety. And these mentors can also prove to be a fountain of ideas and a force for change as they get to know the pupils in their care.

Neston High School actually has more than enough evidence to prove the point, having seen dozens of year 7s soar up the attainment ladder after they introduced a mentoring scheme. It was developed as a result of their work with the charity Achievement for All (more of which on pp.81–98) to tackle underachievement in their new intake. Some 40 children were starting school each year with a 4c or below in maths or English (compared to a target of 4b), so the school looked hard at what was holding their year 7s back.

'One of the first things we did was speak to their families. We knew one-to-one English and maths would help, but wasn't going to be enough on its own,' says Neston's assistant head, Kirsty Cunningham.

'What we learned from the parents and carers was that these pupils were struggling socially – with making friends, and getting into a social group – as much as they were struggling with their studies. They were nervous about things that we might have taken for granted – mixing with older students, getting homework in on time. They needed more than help with English and maths; they needed a structure that would help them settle in and build confidence.'

And this is how Neston's mentoring programme was born, and why it now supports scores of students in the school on an ongoing basis. Between 35 and 40 year 7s are assigned mentors for two years from the time of arrival in school, one mentor to two students or – if that student mentee needs extra support, two mentors to one mentee. And all children can benefit from mentoring via more targeted groups as they move up the school (and face issues such as exam pressure or more specific social difficulties).

What makes a mentor?

While mentoring is more than an arbitrary friendship (it's not enough to direct kids in assembly to 'look out for each other') it's not designed to be a counselling service. Mentoring works best when it's seen as a cool, positive service, rather than a potentially stigmatising need for help. Mentors have to be trained (and this must cover safeguarding training so they know when to call in adult help), but are there to listen. Their greatest asset is empathy; this of course is an asset that can benefit them as well as their mentee as they move into adulthood. And their greatest skill is the ability to hear and not dismiss feelings. Crucially they can help a school 'normalise' talking about fears and anxieties, and so help make mental health matter. Schools who might suggest children must 'learn how to stand on their own two feet and negotiate friendships on their own' should know that mentoring actually helps children to better manage their own emotions and problems. Evidence from mentoring schemes suggests increased attendance, integration and attainment.

'What it recognises is that friendship is often the most important thing in a young person's life,' says Kirsty. 'As they're going through high school, being valued by a peer group can feel as important as being part of a family – more important sometimes. If a student's unhappy at school, it is usually because they are isolated and lonely. It is often because of something that has happened with their friends or classmates.' Neston was determined to create a community where those needs were met, using mentors not to fill the friendship gap but to help mentees build their confidence and so fit more easily into their own peer group.

Neston High already had a leadership programme – groups of year 10 and 11 pupils who were doing well, had good relationships with each other and the staff, and who the school knew were good role models. They just weren't being used as mentors. So the school trained them. 'Initially we just took them off the timetable for a day and looked at issues an underachieving year 7 pupil might be facing,' says Kirsty. 'We did lots of role play, working through likely situations in and out of class. The training included the same safeguarding training we give our staff. And then one Monday morning we introduced them to our target group.'

Now mentors and mentees meet every Monday morning for half an hour. The mentors – prepped by teachers overseeing the project – take a different theme to their mentees to start the session off (homework, friendship, revision, lunchtimes). They talk through issues, set targets, and look back at the week just gone and chat about anything else on the mentee's mind. Outside the Monday morning session, mentors know to look out for their mentees, and might hang out at break, or walk home from school with them if they want to talk.

In this way, mentors tune into and pick up on issues that might be holding their young charges back. 'For example, mentors brought to us their concern about lunchtime clubs,' says Kirsty. The school has all sorts of lunchtime 'eXL clubs', from film to sport to poetry, but the mentors noticed that their mentees weren't signing up and so were missing out. They'd also discovered it was usually because they didn't have friends to go with, or that their mentees assumed club members would all be from older years. 'That's when the mentors set up an eXL taster day, where they introduced the year 7s to the club, going along with them, and then organised a lunch for them all to discuss what they'd found. Over 70 per cent signed up for a club the following week, and started to benefit from all it offered.'

Kirsty sees a different type of student after just a term of mentoring. 'They're less fearful of the older students, more confident in class. And that translates into results – the initial impetus for the scheme,' she says, explaining that combining mentoring with the more focused attention on studies saw students making, on average, 1.7 years of reading age progress in six weeks. 'It astounded us to start with, but now it's the norm. Making children feel happy and confident to come to school simply elevated their ability to make progress. We have the results to prove that every year.'

They are the kind of results grabbing the government's attention. Early in 2016 they put out a call for evidence, seeking the feedback of young people, their parents, and professionals in the healthcare and educational arena about mentoring. And they brought together a series of schools who've made mentoring work to look at a best practice model that could be shared. Those workshops underlined the importance of having a leadership team who bought into the scheme and assigned staff to support and supervise its progress. They also demonstrated the need for a recruitment process to ensure the right students are signing up as mentors, and a pastoral support structure so issues arising from mentoring can be quickly addressed (rather than mentoring working as a stand-alone programme).

Helen Newman from Sandon School, a large comprehensive in Chelmsford, Essex, was at the workshops presenting what she'd found from a ten-year peer support programme.

'It started at Sandon with the realisation that there just weren't enough staff to go round to meet the needs of the pupils in the school, but that there was a resource – a source of resilience building – in the students higher up in the school years. A resource that would be easy to tap into,' explains Newman.

At Sandon, the mentors – and there are 150 at any one time, recruited from years 10 to 13 – receive initial training at a peer mentoring day during the summer term. This is composed of a number of workshops, led by staff or volunteer visiting professionals who can raise awareness of some of the pressures young people face, and obstacles including mental health issues that can develop. This year they've welcomed a police liaison officer, therapeutic counsellors and specialists from CAMHS (child and adolescent mental health services) to help run the sessions.

'Safeguarding is always part of this and mentors know when to call in help from staff at the school. But the training is about teaching them to listen, about how to start conversations (we might role play during these sessions) and about equipping them with skills and strategies to support the students they mentor,' says Newman.

Later, at the start of each new school year, the mentors are separated into teams. One, the 'Here to Help' team, targets pupils with short-term issues such as fallings-out in the playground. 'They're great at noticing things and stepping in before a problem escalates,' says Newman. 'And they've helped other students become more aware of peers, to the point where it's not unusual for a student who isn't even a peer mentor to stop a teacher in the corridor and say "I think Simon in year 8 is having a bit of an issue with something," and to talk about what they've witnessed and are worried about.'

Sometimes Sandon will put a group of mentors around an individual who is struggling (as a result of anything from bereavement to bullying), and they also have groups – rather like in the Neston model – who will be assigned to help tackle issues as they arise. 'We have academic mentors to help pupils with their work, including those who are struggling, but also those who are very able and want to be challenged and nurtured,' explains Newman. 'We also have groups set up to tackle issues as they arise. We had a group helping children negotiate cyber issues and social media, and one term, when we had a group of lads who'd brought issues with them from primary and who were at risk of being too disruptive, we set up a group of mentors called the

"Boys will be Boys" who worked with them, while they worked through their issues.'

Sandon School is known as a very caring school, she says, and she believes that's come from the students themselves, their way of operating. 'That's not to say no child will ever experience unkindness. But what mentors give children is confidence to address the issues that they meet,' says Newman.

One of the ways Sandon measures the success of the programme is via the number of students who want to be part of the mentoring scheme. 'We know it adds something special to the mentors' education. Very often they're pupils who have been mentored lower down the school themselves, who know the power of that kind of support to promote wellbeing, and want to do the same for others coming up the school. That speaks volumes, doesn't it?'

In My View

Nicky Cox on a campaign to get children talking

Nicky Cox, MBE is a journalist and editor-in-chief of *First News*, the newspaper aimed at children and teenagers.

I learn with every issue of *First News* that children need to know their voice is as important as the voice of teachers, politicians and world leaders. That they too, can make a difference. We poll readers every week to get their opinion about things, and we put those opinions in front of world leaders for them. We can get a quarter of a million signatures backing campaigns on everything from child soldiers to refugees.

If we are going to tackle mental health we have to start talking and listening to the young people we are trying to help. They have to be part of any conversation – we need a bottom-up rather than top-down approach.

Children and teenagers may be stuck in the middle of this issue, but they also understand the complexities of what's going on: how the selfie culture and social networking make them feel, how communication between them is breaking down, how words can be misinterpreted, how their self-worth can be shaped by how many likes they get on a picture, how problems like exam pressure and bullying sabotage lives.

If we can help children and young people identify and understand the problems they're experiencing we can bring them back into the conversation and learn from them what the solutions might be, and help them help themselves – and each other.

We are launching a campaign with Heads Together, a coalition of mental health charities, working with Princes William and Harry and Catherine, the Duchess of Cambridge. The intention is to make mental health something that people talk about, rather than brush under the carpet. As I write this today, a new study has been published which reports that one in three boys will not talk about their mental health, even when prompted to by their fathers. Talking about how we feel mentally should be as natural as talking about how we feel physically. We hope our campaign makes that happen.

2

The LEGO® Club

Building Communication Skills and Confidence, One Brick at a Time

For children who find it difficult to socialise
with others, and fit into the group, there is a
tool – and a quite brilliant toy – that could help.
Daniel LeGoff, the man who developed LEGO-
based therapy, invites you to start building.

'For children with social communication difficulties…you can't force a change by telling them how to behave, or by putting them with a group and expecting positive behaviour to be reinforced. That's like putting a child with a hearing impairment in a class of hearing children in the hope it will reinforce good hearing. It's just not going to happen.'

DR DANIEL LEGOFF

The first thing you hear when you walk into this classroom at Manchester's Grange School today is the satisfying sound of LEGO bricks being clicked together. Around each table three sets of eyes focus on the form they are creating, knowing the infinite possibilities laid out before them on the table. But perhaps sweetest of all – even if it's less obvious, even to those taking part – is the sense of each child being part of a team as they work together to build their multi-coloured creations.

Today, here in Manchester, LEGO®-based therapy is working its magic and it has everything and nothing to do with these age-old coloured bricks. The children in this room are here to learn how to communicate with each other; the bricks piled on their tables are simply a bridge between them, a common passion, and the reason they want to come here every week to build something new.

Move closer and it's clear that each pupil in each group has a role. One takes on the job of engineer, instructing others what piece of LEGO is needed and where it has to go, the next the supplier who finds the piece and delivers it to the third child – the builder – who is putting the whole thing together.

'And as they go they're building key communication skills – how to negotiate and solve problems together, interact with and accommodate each other,' explains Rachel Samuels, a speech and language specialist at Grange Special School in Manchester. 'It's raising the pupils' awareness of each other and helping them develop social perspective-taking skills (such as joint attention and consideration of others' points of view) as well as language. I've been a speech therapist for many years but only came across LEGO-based therapy a few years ago and I am completely bowled over by the power of it. All the social skill lessons in the world can't deliver learning like this where the children are feeling frustrations and sorting them out, understanding their place in the group and how to be a positive part of it, while achieving goals and celebrating those achievements.'

The superpower of LEGO was discovered almost by accident by Canadian child neuropsychologist Dr Daniel LeGoff after he witnessed an inadvertent conversation between two eight-year-old children in his clinic. They had coincidentally brought LEGO creations with them that day and as one was leaving and the other was arriving, LeGoff says they discovered each other. Both boys had Asperger's syndrome and hadn't shown any interest in each other (or indeed in other children in general) prior to this moment in the clinic, adds LeGoff. However, after a discussion with their parents and when given the opportunity to play LEGO® together, they didn't hesitate. 'At their first LEGO-based therapy session the two boys were using social skill-building strategies such as sharing, turn-taking, making eye contact and using each other's names,' says LeGoff. 'Within months of deciding to run a club based on the principles I had 70 referrals and before long nine groups running.'

The idea that was born, and Dr Dan (as LeGoff became known to children) went on to pioneer with colleagues in the US and the UK, is now used across the world. Both in classrooms for children with autistic spectrum disorders like those at Manchester's Grange School and for thousands of others whose social communication difficulties result from issues ranging from depression to dyslexia, neglect to attachment disorder, bullying to under-achievement. Issues which get in the way of friendships, learning, attainment and employment and, crucially, their sense of worth to others and the schools and communities where they're based.

What makes LEGO special?

LEGO, it seems, proves to be the perfect toy. Not only for children across the world (and it's reckoned there are now over 60 pieces of LEGO for every person on the planet) but for children who struggle to fit into that world. It offers both limitless possibilities (especially with the plethora of new figures and scenarios) but within the limits LEGO demands (everyone clicks bricks together in the same way, which minimises unease about players' talent levels). At the same time, it works for a broad age and skill range, allowing some to work wonders by following instructions with basic bricks, easily undoing mistakes and exploring other ways to make a model work, while older or more able groups might start to design their own masterpieces using smaller and more complex pieces and figures. Go into any LEGO® store and check out the kids (from toddlers to teens) gathered shoulder to shoulder round the play tables to illustrate the point. For them all, LEGO always provides evidence of their creativity and teamwork, both for their own benefit and in order to demonstrate it to others.

Crucially, adds LeGoff, it can appeal to children with a whole range of interests. While you could take the nub of the idea (children having different roles, working together) and apply it to building train tracks or baking cakes, LEGO crosses play 'continents' and opens up a whole world of online clubs, movies and video games children can enjoy as they progress.

'I once had a boy come along who didn't want to play LEGO at all,' says LeGoff. 'His interest was the weather. He was fascinated by it. So I suggested he build a LEGO weather station, and even do a weather report from the station via a mini video. He took that back to his group and they ended up doing a whole news report, including the weather with a LEGO studio backdrop.'

Making it work in your school

Make no mistake, this isn't about dumping buckets of bricks on tables for children to play with at lunchtime while adults sit by drinking coffee. LEGO-based therapy is effectively a collaborative play therapy bringing children together to build models. The sessions make a difference because the groups – always carefully matched – are able to learn how to work with each other. Each depends on the adults leading the sessions – and they are as vital as the bricks themselves – knowing the individual children and the basic rules of the LEGO-based therapy game. Crucially, they must facilitate the process (making sure groups are well matched, everyone gets their turn, disputes don't get out of hand, no one disrupts or disturbs others' games, etc.) but not interfere with it. The adult supervisors are there to help create and maintain a space where children can learn the rights and wrongs of social engagement and how to work through the tussles of relationships without having to deal with the distress of being ignored (or worse) in an unsupervised group or playground setting.

Achieving that balance can be hard for staff, says LeGoff. 'When I bring in my own students to help I have to stop them getting too involved,' he explains. 'They might want to protect the child or help them when they're struggling, but the whole point of this is giving children the chance to learn for themselves. To work out their own responses and solutions as the team works together.'

In LeGoff's view these sessions offer kids a team, in the same way sport might if they played football or rugby. 'Many children who benefit from LEGO® therapy don't like or aren't good at sport and suffer at school as a result,' he says. 'LEGO play can bring all the benefits they'd get from being on a sports team. The adults leading the sessions have to act as a coach-cum-referee. And a coach who sees a player struggling doesn't go on the pitch and kick the ball for them.'

There are other key rules, drawn from LeGoff's own experience and the therapists and teachers who've taken LEGO-based therapy on board and shared what they've found. They range from avoiding artificial social rules (such as shaking hands) to keeping parents out of the club so children learn to bond with their teammates. They go from making sure the LEGO projects are big enough to challenge but small enough to finish in the session (to avoid frustration and disappointment). They specify that LEGO 'teams' must be selected carefully (in the same way a football team might be) to ensure a good fit.

It's called LEGO® club because another rule of the game is this is never called therapy – and so not stigmatised. And teamwork is crucial. Children might initially come wanting and expecting to play on their own, but in these sessions they work in pairs, threes or fours. The LEGO challenge at hand is achieved by the children taking on interdependent roles (as illustrated at Grange School earlier) so communication – verbal and non-verbal – is needed to complete the build. There are a whole number of ways it can be developed and used – from games involving just an adult and one child, to games involving two peers, to more freestyle collaborative set building. These are known as LEGO-based therapy 'models' – check out the panel on pp.38–39 for more information.

'We know that children learn as a result of relationships – with their peers they work with, with the role models they look up to, and the teachers they want to do well for,' says LeGoff. 'If you don't care about relationships, or fall foul of bad ones, the motivation for learning disappears. Good teachers get that, but even the best ones can get distracted by the pressures of the curriculum.

'For children showing autistic type behaviour or demonstrating other social communication difficulties – which often means they struggle to "get" other people – you can't force a change in that by *telling* them how to behave, or just by putting them with a group and expecting positive behaviour to be reinforced,' says LeGoff. 'That's like putting a child with a hearing impairment in a class of hearing children in the hope it will reinforce good hearing. It's just not going to happen.' Which is why, he asserts, children on the autistic spectrum, or children who struggle with social communication for other reasons, can just drop out of other social groups at school and end up wandering around on the edge of the playground, staring out the window wishing they were somewhere else, or kicking off, frustrated by what they are feeling. 'Then a secondary level of resistance appears – from the social anxiety they're experiencing as a result of not fitting in,' says LeGoff.

This isn't, though, just about fitting in or having friends in the playground, although that clearly emerges from LEGO®-based therapy, and has a huge impact on children's wellbeing and so learning. But LeGoff has his eye on the bigger picture. 'The kind of social communication I'm interested in is not about making friends, but about helping children *function* in groups. I know when they can do the latter, friendships often develop and that's great,' he says. 'I've seen this happen in my own clinics. But what alarms me is that you have intelligent, creative children going through school and the lack of social skills and resulting isolation not only impacts on them (and their learning) while they're there, but more so when they leave. They don't get jobs or promotions because they are socially awkward and unable to communicate clearly. If they do get a job they can end up stuck in their cubicle at work every lunchtime because they don't know how to chit-chat and no one wants to grab lunch or a coffee with them. They can't communicate their ideas effectively, or properly collaborate and work as a team. That is what limits them.'

LeGoff knows we'd all like to be in a world that understands and accepts people with autism and other social difficulties. He recognises things are improving, but is also well aware that in reality there is still much stigma and a lack of understanding of these social communication problems. Think about the number of NEETs (young people Not in Education, Employment or Training) in the UK and the number of kids in the US (where LeGoff is based) who, he says, 'end up playing video games in their parents' basement because they can't get into work'.

'The impact on them, their potential for relationships and work and ultimately their mental health costs society dear,' says LeGoff.

Which brings him back to the schools and how LEGO-based therapy can help. Teachers, he says, even the best ones, can see friendships as something that happen naturally, and which are beyond the classroom and/or their control. They miss the fact that kids who struggle aren't on their own because they want to be, but because they've been surfing the playground saying hello to groups and trying to join in but not succeeding. 'Ten 15-second conversations don't add up to any sort of friendship,' says LeGoff. 'The behaviour shown by these children – their not understanding others – causes other kids to switch off. Teachers might assume others are being polite (they know the child's name, and may acknowledge them), but perhaps don't see how those same children also find these kids annoying and learn to avoid them, believing them self-absorbed or rude.' But in the LEGO® room the children who struggle can learn the rules of the game, and other kids can be brought in to work with them (as mentors, for example) and learn more about their peers and how they operate.

This is where team selection comes into its own. Teachers know only too well that sometimes the apparently 'cool' kids in the class can be the meanest ones, and they're not a good mix with those who most benefit from LEGO-based therapy. Nor are they a good representation of the real life we're preparing them for. 'After all,' LeGoff says, 'the middle school *Lord of the Flies* behaviour is not the real world, and that kind of bullying would get them fired in a future role.

'You want kids who create a realistic model of an adult social setting,' says LeGoff. 'Inclusive, kind but sometimes demonstrating tough love. They help children in the sessions learn what is acceptable and not acceptable by being in positive relationships; not by being on the end of bad ones.'

Of course children might not see, or even be aware of, the benefits as they grow. David and Miles, both graduates of the LEGO club at their comprehensive near Cardiff, say that what they value most is the friendships that grew out of it. They now meet with three other boys from the club on Saturdays to play LEGO® games, or to make their own mini LEGO-themed movies on their iPads.

'But that did make the whole of school better,' says Miles. 'I was in the SEN group for English and Maths because I'm dyslexic and have ADD. I wasn't making friends there, and I was rubbish at footie so had nothing to do at lunchtime. Suddenly, when they launched LEGO club, I had somewhere to hang out every Tuesday and Thursday, and mates who seemed to understand me the other times. I liked that. People stopped winding me up and teasing me, just because I am rubbish at football. And yes, I guess I am doing well at school now.'

In Rachel Samuel's LEGO club in Manchester, she allows time for some self-reflection, where children can talk about what they were most proud of in the session. 'I kept my cool when he was being really slow building' or 'I helped her when she was struggling to find a brick.' Samuel recognises that in her setting – 174 children who aren't terribly good at accommodating each other because of their autism – the gradual development from working with an adult to working in a pair might not be necessary in mainstream. But the skills that are developed (patience, communication, compromise, role swapping) are, she says, crucial for all children.

'The idea of being able to put differences aside and work on something together is so positive. There is something emotionally regulating about it,' she says. As well as using it in classroom-type sessions Grange School has lunchtime clubs for children who know the rules of the club and who come together (still with adults to facilitate) to build things around a theme. That might be models with wheels this week, and buildings next time.

'We had a couple of lads who'd become best friends through LEGO club but were struggling to maintain the friendship,' says Samuel. 'We took them back to simple builds to help them check in with each other. Those sessions helped them understand each other again, and understand their own feelings better and how those feelings, and their actions, were impacting on each other. That, to me, is at the heart of this therapy.'

Samuel – a self-confessed Playmobil girl in her youth – says she is now a convert to LEGO®. 'Nothing on its own revolutionises social interaction. But it is a privilege to watch the power this has,' she says. 'There is an increased respect among fellow builders and fellow pupils, and you can see how it improves their social interactions in and out of the club. A couple of years ago 60 of them were involved in creating the house from *The Simpsons*, working in twos and small groups. It was so cool. There was such a sense of pride in what they'd made, and the way they'd worked together. Who would have thought a pile of bricks could make that kind of difference.'

LEGO®-Based Therapy (Jessica Kingsley Publishers) is a complete guide to this subject and provides schools with everything they need to know to set up and run a LEGO-based club. It shows how, by providing a setting for this play therapy, pupils can learn to share, take turns, make eye contact and follow social rules, bringing benefits that spill over into friendships and classroom learning, and so their social confidence and self-esteem.

The book's written by Daniel LeGoff who discovered and pioneered the idea, Dr Gina Gomez de la Cuesta, a psychologist and trained teacher who has evaluated the way it works in her research at University of Cambridge Autism Research Centre, Simon Baron-Cohen, Professor of Developmental

Psychopathology at the University of Cambridge and Director, Autism Research Centre, and Dr GW Krauss, a psychologist who has worked on the development and implementation of LEGO®-based therapy with Daniel LeGoff.

In order for LEGO-based therapy to work effectively in schools to promote social communication and emotional wellbeing, it is essential that the clubs are supervised by adults who have understood and can apply the researched method of play. This is outlined clearly in the book, which also includes input from other teachers who have tried and tested LEGO clubs in a mainstream and special school setting.

The National Autistic Society has a whole range of information and publications that can not only help individuals with autism, but also help their families and staff in schools understand the condition and how they can better support children on the spectrum.

A group of the charity's young campaigners have helped the NAS launch a charter to improve understanding of their mental health needs. Called *You Need to Know*, it is designed for mental health practitioners, including those based at CAMHS.

For more information about autism, the young campaigners' charter and a number of services the NAS can offer to promote children's mental health in schools, visit www.autism.org.uk.

In My View

Jane Asher on the campaign to understand autism and mental health

Actress and author Jane Asher has been president of the National Autistic Society for over 30 years. The charity wants to raise awareness of the number of children on the spectrum who suffer mental health problems, and the measures schools and health professionals can take to prevent this and to help promote their emotional wellbeing.

We know everyday life for children and young people with autism can be confusing and even frightening. Many of them find understanding and communicating with others particularly difficult, which can leave them vulnerable to bullying or to feeling isolated and even worthless to their peer group. As a result, children with autism are often described as being 'loners' as if that is their choice when in fact it is sometimes their way of coping. This can be counter-productive, leaving them feeling more low and more anxious.

It's no surprise then that mental health problems are more common in children and young people with autism than in the general population. They are, at the same time, often overlooked or considered unavoidable. The National Autistic Society (NAS) challenges this view, claiming that while more than seven out of ten children with autism also have a mental health problem (one in ten of children who access CAMHS each year are on the autistic spectrum) and differences inherent in the condition can play a part, it is the social difficulties that can sabotage their self-esteem and feelings of emotional wellbeing. This is something we must address.

The NAS believes that many of the social problems children with autism face could be avoided by using initiatives that promote communication and peer connectedness, and LEGO®-based therapy is a good example. The NAS has a wealth of information and advice to help schools with initiatives like this, and my favourite part of this job – as President of the NAS – is going into those schools and seeing the difference that support makes. Seeing the improvement in children's confidence and ability to make friends, and their parents' happiness when their children are given the chance to play and learn alongside others, and to feel understood and that they are a valued part of the class.

We can all play a part in ensuring young people with autism feel valued and understood. Over the years, having worked with and watched so many children and adults with autism, and made many friends with an ASD, I have come to value much in the autistic way of interacting with the world, which I would rather see as a different, rather than 'wrong', way of being. I think parents whose children aren't affected by these issues might be surprised how much they'd get out of supporting youngsters in their own child's class who are struggling because they have autism. I think they would be surprised at how much their own children would learn from those new relationships, too.

3

The Perfect Week

Introducing the Head Teacher Whose Out of the Box Thinking Is Changing Children's Lives

There are some astounding head teachers in the UK, making children's mental health their priority. We went to meet one of them, on a mission to discover what would make a perfect week for his students and to show how some out of the box thinking can shape their success.

'We could say we don't have the resources to deal with this, or that we haven't the time to address it. But if we fall back on those arguments we won't change anything. We won't give these kids the skills they need to make a good life for themselves in the future.'

PAUL GREEN, HEAD TEACHER, LYNG HALL

In the school hall at Lyng Hall Comprehensive in Coventry, pupils and their families are milling around a marketplace of tables, talking to stall holders and each other as they go. The stall holders are not selling crafts, raising funds, promoting GCSE subjects or pushing careers, however. Nor indeed are they doing any of the things you'd usually find in school halls like this one. Instead, they are here to promote mental health, and more specifically what part they might play in promoting mental health in this school, this week. There are school nurses, police liaison officers, social care teams, youth services, children Family First workers, and voluntary organisations such as Citizens Advice, Mind and Compass.

This is part of the school's Perfect Week, an idea they've borrowed from the NHS and which involves imagining what a perfect week would look like – not by ignoring the problems, but by trying out new ideas and behaviours so they can find better ways to tackle them.

Lyng Hall's head teacher, Paul Green, has adopted the scheme for his school and today he wants to see what happens when families are introduced to the help that's out there, so that when they hit trouble they can find support faster and benefit from interventions earlier. Paul would, he says, like to find a permanent fixture for this kind of hub, but that will have to wait for another day. As he circulates, he presses for more interaction between tables, wanting to see the professionals in the room, including his own staff, share ideas with each other as well as the families, so they can reduce needless overlap and subsequent delays delivering help.

'For as long as I've been a head teacher I've heard colleagues in schools and agencies outside them wishing they could all work more closely,' says Green. 'They recognise the mental health issues children face, and want to help prevent them. They recognise how this impacts on their learning and their future.' He sees the market stalls today as a way of getting that ball rolling – testing ideas, starting new conversations and exploring ways of collaborating.

By way of example, Green points to social workers, in school today to shadow his teaching staff. 'This is giving them a different perspective of how we work. They had imagined lessons – everyone imagines lessons when they think of school – but had no idea of what we did in between times to link up with families or to tackle issues children are facing.' Next, he wants to see his teaching staff shadowing social workers so they can understand their work better. This will help the school see 'how they connect and support families, and understand why they have such high thresholds for interventions'.

Green reckons there is a need to build professional trust. 'I can already see from this first exercise how we can help social workers; by giving them more understanding of the pupils and the work we've done here to support them. This can save them time, as well as overlaps. And I can see how the social care team can contribute to our educational outcomes. In the same way if we're working with housing charities – we can line them up with what we know is happening, and via earlier intervention make sure housing issues don't impact on children's lives and so schooling.'

Green knows how busy everyone is, and how the problems of limited staff and limited resources are endemic. 'There's a lot of high-end fire-fighting and less time for initiatives that prevent problems escalating,' he says. 'During the Perfect Week we'll be sitting down as a group of professionals and looking at cases we've all been involved with. We want to go back and try to identify the first signs that something was wrong, and take what we learn from that exercise and map it onto existing families. This will help us understand what might be going on for the child who can't cope socially or is often absent or always late. If we can work out what the warning signs are we can – if we work together – prevent things becoming a bigger problem. The solution is always simpler and more effective the earlier we implement it.'

He has his work cut out. Lyng Hall sits in the centre of an enormous housing estate on the outskirts of Coventry and serves the most socio-economically challenged area of the city. Nearly half his pupils come from Eastern Europe, don't speak English as a first language and are trying to settle into a new community and make it their home. The life expectancy in this catchment is ten years less than a more affluent part of the city. 'That's a problem that starts at birth and not at 40,' says Green. 'If their health is such a problem that they are more likely to die early than kids ten miles down the road, that must affect their ability to learn.'

A different kind of outcome and ambition

'We could say we don't have the resources to deal with this, or that we haven't the time to address it,' he adds. 'But if we fall back on those arguments we won't change anything. We won't give these kids the skills they need to make a good life for themselves in the future. Schools can too easily categorise children – rich, poor, SEN, academic. But they are all children and they are all going to have some sort of challenge to get the best of outcomes, and in my eyes the best of outcomes is to become kind, responsible adults. We want to do all we can to help them towards that outcome.'

So no, Paul Green is not obsessed with academic results and he jokes that it's remarkable, given this, that he's still in a job. But he's clearly a man who likes to think out of the box, as illustrated by the list of other ideas he's brought to the staff room table in the run up to the Perfect Week. He hit the headlines some time ago when he opened a Citizen's Advice Bureau at the school and had teachers trained to become CAB staff, an initiative one parent credited with preventing homelessness, another with saving her life. And there are scores more stories like this one, with a weight and impact on children that we'll never see measured in league tables.

How kindness rules

Green's belief that kindness is at the heart of all he does and is, crucially, one of the greatest ways to promote his pupils' emotional wellbeing translates into staff guidelines that now include rules on never shouting at children, never using the word detention ('we adhere to a positive rather than punitive method of discipline') and having an open door to parents who can raise concerns anytime, and well before they become big issues. During summer exams he invested a huge amount of time organising and training his team so pupils who might feel overwhelmed by a huge exam hall could sit the papers in smaller rooms and groups, a three-week logistical nightmare to help children feel more at ease.

'The first thing I expect my staff to do is smile and tell the students how much they're looking forward to teaching them,' he says. 'If they have a bad lesson, I don't want them to react to the child. The first thing I want them to think about is what they did or didn't do (or didn't know) that allowed that to happen. And I want them to share that in the staff room, because when they do, the staff here want to help. They might talk through the lesson, or go in and help with the next one. They help each other become better teachers.'

'Detentions', when they're needed, are translated into 'extra help' and Green or one of his team will talk to the student about why things are not going so well and invite them to stay behind for 'period 6' to catch up, or talk through what went wrong. He'll then ask the pupil to ring their parent or carer and say they have offered to stay behind and catch up. He applies the same principle to lunchtimes when students might need more supervision (read time out from free play) when he invites them to sit down with 'someone who can chat to you about what's going on'. The dinner table that welcomes these teenagers is simply marked as 'reserved'. Look across the canteen and other teachers are dotted around the tables, eating and chatting with pupils, while those in a more supervisory role have walkie-talkies, picking up messages about kids who've come unstuck or are hanging out on their own and may need a helping hand as they come in for lunch.

Social media is also on the hit list. 'My big fear is that children who need help are getting advice from other children on social media, who don't have the right experience or skills to give that advice, and may have all sorts of agendas,' he explains. His response was to introduce a social media tool called Edmodo, which allows teachers to chat online with pupils about homework and other school-related issues, and where those pupils can chat and collaborate with each other. 'We really want them to get used to being in a more responsible forum online, and being more mindful about messages they exchange.'

When Green became head he replaced teaching assistants and learning mentors with a team of associate teachers – a diverse bunch of those (existing but newly trained) teaching assistants, recent graduates and newly qualified teachers. They benefit from training in mental health on the job and work in parallel with the teaching team, shadowing and learning from them with the aim of removing barriers to learning for those pupils who struggle. They might do that by addressing social and emotional problems, working with smaller groups, or supporting parents and carers if they're dealing with difficult behaviour at home, or with adult problems (debt, housing, relationships) that will clearly impact on the child.

'When we launched this idea we wanted every member of staff to have a special connection with students, and we wanted students to know there was a particular person looking out for them,' he says. It was on the back of this that Lyng Hall's attendance started to soar. Some associate teachers stayed in post, championing the students they came to know, while others (including his current head of sixth form) moved on from being an associate and trained as a teacher. 'And they go on to be amazing teachers,' says Green. He tells the story of a boy whose behaviour one day became so poor – he knocked over a teacher in class – that permanent exclusion had to be considered, however reluctantly. 'I was explaining to the pupil about why we had to exclude him when the teacher who'd been at the rough end of the incident came in and asked to speak to me. He'd been chatting with the other staff and they'd worked out a way the pupil could be excluded *within* school rather than having to leave and attend a pupil referral unit. The staff had agreed to teach him in their free lessons, and to help him work through the issues he was dealing with,' says Green. 'I want staff who care that much, and I love it that they do. Sometimes they tell me that families have contacted them out of school, on one occasion to help start a broken down car. I love it that families trust us that much.'

The majority of staff – as they graduate from one post to the other – stay at Lyng Hall, and the low staff turnover is one of the reasons Green describes his budget as healthy. That and the fact his associate teacher team can provide cover (removing the need for supply). He says that while they value the property and the resources within it – and it's a bright, beautiful place to be – the building is not their top priority. 'Kids learn more when the relationships with staff are right. That's what matters.'

When pressed about where his approach was born, he says that when he was a student, he was the trainee teacher more interested in child psychology than anything else. Yet his quiet confidence and commitment is clearly something that has grown with a love of the job and the pupils who turn up at his gate each day. Attendance is 96 per cent, which is exceptional in its own right and especially given the number of children from immigrant families new to the country (who average attendance at around

75 per cent elsewhere in the UK). It's those keen pupils who continually prompt him to come up with new ways to reach them and to make them smile.

'I am liberated by my exam results,' he says wryly (which show 34 per cent of his students receiving five A*–C GCSE grades at the time of writing, compared to the 80 per cent heads want to boast about). 'We know why those results are low. We have hundreds of children who are only just learning to speak English and need to dissect a piece of text and answer cryptic questions about it using language their peers have had for 16 years. We have hundreds of children who might be facing hugely difficult family issues at home. They bring with them all sorts of anxieties and concerns about life. Will their mum be around when they get home? Will their dad have a job? Will they have a home or will they have been evicted?'

But those results, and the reasons behind them, make it imperative to try new things to improve outcomes, says Green, who believes his current campaign – via the Perfect Week – will help them do just that.

'Many of the ways the education system measures success are more challenging for my kids. But what we are doing is working. We look at our attendance, and at the increase in numbers going to university each year. We look at the fact that one of our kids has won an award for her science studies, and at the way the children welcome visitors and treat each other. But for some, mere survival is a measure of their success. For us, seeing those children want to come back every day, and leave when the bell goes with a smile on their face is enough.' At least, he adds with another smile, 'it is this week'.

Young Minds is a charity working to improve the emotional wellbeing and mental health of children and young people. Their website offers resources for parents, young people and schools. They offer schools free, practical resources to help everyone in schools support pupils' emotional wellbeing and academic resilience. For more information visit www. youngminds.org.uk.

MindEd offers free educational resources containing advice on the most common ways that mental health problems appear in children and young adults and detailed practical ways to support adults who want to help. Visit www.minded.org.uk.

In My View

Jane Powell on the campaign to
address male suicide, and how
your school could help

Jane Powell is founder and CEO of CALM (The Campaign
Against Living Miserably), which works to prevent male suicide
in the UK. It is also one of the partner charities working with
Heads Together, which aims to change the national conversation
on mental wellbeing.

One in four of us will have mental health problems. That's what
the figures show, but I believe we should think in terms of four
in four. We all have inner lives; we all face problems. There is
an 'us and them' about the one in four, which isn't helpful at all
and which adds to the stigma of mental illness. There needs to
be a push back that says this issue is about all of us – and about
children, too.

Take the shocking level of suicide among young men – the
single biggest killer of men aged 45 and under. Our charity is
specifically trying to address this.

There are two things we have to tackle. First there is a stigma
which prevents people talking about suicide. Those left behind
have to deal with the shock and grief and may feel implicated
and even ashamed. Those who feel suicidal may believe they are
inadequate in some way; that they have failed, or that they haven't
got the stuffing for life.

Second we're dealing with sexism. While we're rightly sensitive to sexist remarks directed at women, we happily allow boys and men to be told they should 'man up' or 'strap on a pair' or that they're 'crying like a big girl'. Our society is imbued with the idea that the very definition of a man is strength. Men are meant to be the strong ones, looking after others – not vulnerable, not 'at risk'. So it's no surprise that even those men who talk about depression, too often discuss it with an element of shame and embarrassment.

Given that grown men find it hard to go against the grain and talk about their own feelings, how much harder must it be for boys?

We need to tackle these two problems and break that cycle of thinking as a matter of urgency. And schools have a key opportunity to help us do this.

I'd like to see lessons in what it really means to live as a teenager, so young people understand what is happening to them. As adults, we understand the issues around those teenage years – the peer pressure and hormone surges, the ongoing development (of brain and body) and the incredible stress of schooling. But do teenagers understand what's going on? I don't think they do. Many of them don't get that book until they're in their 20s, or are parents themselves. So what's the best way forward?

Teenagers are constantly on a journey of exploration and trying to work out if they're normal and how they fit in. But they are also subject to an intense amount of self-criticism and often an intense amount of peer pressure. Add in hormones and you have a perfect toxic mix that can cause their internal dialogue to spiral out of control and lead them to the wrong place: 'I am rubbish and ugly and will never get a girlfriend... My mum hates me and I am always doing everything wrong... I'll never pass this exam or get a job... I'm a failure.'

Teenagers need to understand what's happening – how their brain is developing, how their hormones are making them feel, and what that intense pressure is doing to their feelings. They also need to understand that everyone is likely to have mental health issues at some point and to understand what depression looks like. Then, when they hit a dark point in their life they will recognise what is happening, and know where to get help. Or, when their friends hit that point they will know how to respond.

I'd like to see teachers talking about their own feelings and their own mental health in these lessons. Otherwise it can too easily become a lesson that kids sit through believing the teacher doesn't really understand the feelings they dare not share. They believe the teacher can't possibly understand what they are going through – issues with parents, bullying, relationships, or worries about the size of their ears, their yearning for sex, the changes in their body. What a relief it would be for them to hear about their teachers' own struggles as teenagers, and now. How can young people feel comfortable talking about their feelings if teachers don't want to?

The Heads Together campaign launched recently by Prince Harry and the Duke and Duchess of Cambridge works in partnership with a group of charities, including ours. We want to tackle the source of this issue, and to enable boys to support each other early on and change the way society supports them. But we know just talking isn't enough. To nail this issue, we have to go further and make the notion of masculinity bigger, more inclusive and more tolerant. I'd like to see schools provide a space where children can talk about what it means to be a man and what it means to be a woman when it comes to society's expectations, and how those expectations might exacerbate problems for both sexes. Let's make this a positive space for lively debate, separate from any counselling room or pastoral care office, which some might not feel comfortable turning to. Children's perspectives can be exciting and different. Perhaps we can learn something from them that will help us make a real, positive change.

The Campaign Against Living Miserably – or
CALM – is a small charity with big ambitions to
tackle and prevent male suicide in the UK. It offers
support via their helpline and website, and via other
initiatives (such as their own magazine distributed in
Topman). They believe that if men felt able to ask for
help when they needed it, hundreds of suicides could
be prevented. If you'd like to find out more about
their work and resources visit www.thecalmzone.net.

4

The Poem

Exploring the Perfect Starting Point to Talk about Feelings

If poetry takes words and memories and feelings and turns them into art, then a conversation about poetry can take art and turn it into a way to explore our feelings, and what to do about them. Poet and mental health expert Dr Pooky Knightsmith shows you how.

'For me poetry created a window in the day when I was able to take everything I was feeling and put it down on paper...'

DR POOKY KNIGHTSMITH

Just because you do not share
My feelings of anxiety,
Doesn't mean those feelings
Are not there,
Should not be heard.

Just because you do not care
That I feel like I'm drowning,
Doesn't mean those feelings
Are my fault
Or well-deserved.

It is strange how powerful 40-odd words can be. Here in these lines the writer has been able to use a poem to put down feelings she didn't know what else to do with. There is no pressure on them to be right or wrong, good or bad. No need for any understanding of the iambic pentameter or the rules about rhyme. Like any piece of art, if it works for the writer or the person looking at or reading it, it works.

These words – this poem – worked for Dr Pooky Knightsmith, and will work – she hopes – for others now reading it. One of our country's leading experts on mental health, she turned to poems – one a day to be exact – when she was dealing with her own mental health issues and decided to share them when she realised the power of poetry; not only during her own illness and recovery, but to promote good mental health moving forward. The result of this (*Using Poetry to Promote Talking and Healing*) is an extraordinary multifaceted book. At its heart is the idea that poetry can be used as a way into a discussion about difficult feelings, and a means of finding a path through them.

'I had hundreds – I literally wrote one a day – and when I was reading them months later it was like someone else had written them, but it was someone who really got me,' says Knightsmith now. 'I was anxious about sharing them, but mostly felt I'd become an imposter in a world that is not mine. But that's the point I am trying to make. Poetry – and so many forms of art – is a world anyone can embrace and which can do something positive in this arena.'

Using poetry in the classroom

Pooky Knightsmith is not the only mental health expert signposting the role of art (drawing, painting, music, drama, dance) to help children express how they are feeling when more direct explanations or more conventional conversational exchanges don't seem to come easily. And while poetry might be less explored than painting, music or drama, she argues it can help everyone, including children and young people. It can give them a better understanding of where they are now and where they want to be in future. And poetry can, she says, be used to facilitate those other forms of art therapy to build on the benefits. Throughout her book she suggests how a group can be invited to choose music or a favourite track to represent the mood of the poem, or to draw what the poem's subject is feeling (be it panic or sadness, happiness or hope).

'For me poetry created a window in the day when I was able to take everything I was feeling and put it down on paper,' says Knightsmith. 'I wrote them all really quickly – say ten minutes at a time – and I found it so useful I would find myself picking up a pencil or turning to my iPad to write a poem in the moment of anxiety, for example when I was feeling overwhelmed on a crowded train. It dealt with the urgency of the situation. Unlike prose which is often never finished or never quite how you want it, a poem is down and done. Boxed off. And even poems that stay in the box and are never shared can be a source of therapy.'

There are, though, many other benefits that can come out of that metaphorical box. Poems, Knightsmith suggests – including the poems she encourages her readers to write themselves – can be a way to show someone how we're feeling, even if as we write the words, they don't make much sense to us. They can be used to start conversations and open doors to talk about feelings in the third person (for example, as we explore the feelings of the poet, or the person a poem's about) without having to personalise them. Or they can be a way of reflecting about how things are and how we'd like them to be. The book offers a complete anthology (on issues covering abuse and bullying, anxiety, depression, eating disorders and body image, self-harm, supporting and listening to others and more), and brings these practical ideas and applications to life by matching some of the author's own poems with the kind of questions teachers and counsellors could use in a therapeutic setting, in many instances in a class or small group setting in school.

'Obviously the key thing about using them as a teaching tool is choosing poems (mine or other people's) carefully and having appropriate ground rules,' says Knightsmith. So in class sessions teachers would follow a school's normal safeguarding procedures, and it would be important to make it very clear that this is not a session for children to speak out about their own experiences or those of other people (even if poems created in the session are personal). At the same time, it's vital to signpost where children can go for help and, indeed, where any group leaders will be if those children want to talk afterwards.

Starting a conversation: how it might work
FROZEN OUT
She felt lonely,

And alone,

Even when the room was full.

No one wanted to utter her name

For fear of falling foul

Of The Bully.

The Bully had picked her,

Singled her out

As The Victim.

She was special

She supposed,

But she did not feel special.

She felt the pain of redirected eyes

Ceased conversations

Games cut short.

There was no beating,
And no biting,
But this was worse…
She felt alone
When surrounded by those
She once called her friends.

This poem – in Knightsmith's section on bullying and abuse – comes with practical tools and ideas. For example, it's suggested that a class group imagines what the day felt like for the subject of this poem, and what she meant by 'lonely and alone' (can we feel lonely when we are not alone?). What way is the subject special, and what does the group think is happening to her? What, too, does the bully feel?

She matches these with extension activities, for example, by suggesting a group look at different types of bullying and whether one type is more or less bad than another, and where similarities lie. You could, she suggests, invite the group to write a feelings map for the subject, considering how she feels at different points of the day and what can be done to relieve negative feelings and promote positive ones. Or they could be asked to write a letter to the bullies saying all the things the subject wishes she could say, but feels too afraid to speak, as well as writing a list of sources of support the subject can turn to.

Knightsmith also encourages readers to try it out for themselves, offering an easy mini guide to poetic forms to kick start the process – from short three-line Haiku poems and 14-line sonnets in iambic pentameter, to poems in the Anaphora style (using a word or phrase repeated to the start lines) or in pyramid form, varying the length of lines in the poem so it forms a vertical or horizontal pyramid shape.

'Start anywhere,' says Knightsmith, who recognises the barriers children and teachers might foresee – from those who feel they are not skilled to lead a session or write a verse, to those who don't know anything about poetry. 'Be bold, adventurous and feel free to think completely out of the boxes I've used,' she says.

Through her poetry, Knightsmith says she recognised that – despite being incredibly personal to her – great good can come out of sharing a verse, and a journey. As someone who champions mental health and the importance of destigmatising these issues, it seemed only right, she says, to talk about her own journey and one way that helped her through it.

'When you have a mental health issue everyone wants to see you getting better. You have to fight the urge to say you're fine when you're not, just to please them,' she says. 'When you are open and honest about how you feel you not only get the support you need from the people who matter – and they often step up from surprising places – but you also empower other people to be open and honest about how they are feeling too. That can lead to some great discussions in a school, and go towards making everyone more emotionally literate; both for their own sake and also so they can support each other.'

Using Poetry to Promote Talking and Healing by Pooky Knightsmith is published by Jessica Kingsley Publishers and explains how poetry can be a great way to get people talking about difficult issues around mental health. It includes a collection of over 100 poems written by the author with loads of accompanying activities. Visit www.jkp.com for more information.

Using Poetry to Promote Talking and Healing by Pooky Knightsmith is published by Jessica Kingsley Publishers and explains how poetry can be a great way to get people talking about difficult issues around mental health. It includes a collection of over 100 poems written by the author with loads of accompanying activities. Visit www.jkp.com for more information.

Pooky Knightsmith is Vice Chair of the Children and Young People's Mental Health Coalition and Director of the Children, Young People and Schools Programme at the **Charlie Waller Memorial Trust**, which was set up in 1988 in memory of Charlie Waller, a young man who took his own life while suffering from depression. It aims to raise awareness of mental health among young people, to help people recognise the signs of depression in themselves and others, and ensure expert and evidence-based help is available. Their programme for schools and young people provides free evidence-based presentations and training. For more information visit www.cwmt.org.uk.

5

The Anti-Bullying Workshop

Harnessing the Power of Prevention to Promote Inclusion and Build Self-Esteem

Bullying can severely damage mental health, sabotaging young people's self-esteem, schooling and, if left unchecked, future health. At workshops in schools today, the national anti-bullying charity Kidscape is showing teachers what they can do to prevent it.

'Parents and carers who do call on us know that however much they love their kids, and tell them they love them, they cannot always fight the impact of being unloved by their peers. Not only the bullies but by bystanders who've done nothing to help...'

PETER BRADLEY, KIDSCAPE

Sitting in a circle in a stunning 17th century music room, a group of teenagers smile nervously at each other, and with trepidation at the music master sitting in the middle, who has just asked each of them to stand up and sing a solo. This is a big ask. Indeed, this – simply sitting in the company of new friends – is way out of this group's comfort zone to start with. Most are afraid of speaking to the group, but to go beyond this, and to sing…?

Then, slowly, one by one, the teenagers find their voice. For a few, this is just a whisper, with others it's a clear tone, and all are somehow beautiful. Peter Bradley, the residential director, knows how challenging yet rewarding this first activity can be but also how it helps the teenagers get over the first hurdle called trust, essential for the weekend to come.

The teenagers, aged between 14 and 19, are from the broadest mix of backgrounds and schools, each of their stories different from the next. Sixteen in number, they're here for a three-day residential workshop organised by the national anti-bullying charity Kidscape, and supported and hosted by Stowe School in Buckinghamshire. They've been invited here this weekend, though, because they all have one thing in common. They have been brought down so low by bullying at school that they're all dealing with the most serious of mental health problems. Two have already attempted to take their own lives; others have stopped eating, are self-harming or refusing to leave the house alone. One girl has attempted to bleach her black skin white. This evening, and the days ahead, are about giving them a voice, and a place in a group of peers who not only share their experience but also their desire to come back stronger. After the song, each will be challenged to activities ranging from drama to a ropes course, each exercise involving teamwork and trust.

'An onlooker would not believe why they're here,' admits Bradley. 'Especially if they caught the look of complete and utter delight when their peers offer a hand over a climbing wall, welcome them to sit down for lunch, or applaud their efforts in a workshop. It's the stuff all young people need and are nurtured by, but it's been absent from their lives and so feels really special when it comes their way.'

Peter Bradley is director of services at Kidscape, which was the first charity in the UK to fully examine the culture of school bullying. It's at the forefront of new techniques and support – not only advising the government, but also supporting tens of thousands of parents and children who contact the charity each year via its publications, school-based training and anti-bullying workshops. And then there are weekends like this one, designed for those he says are at severe risk of being overwhelmed by the bullying experience and developing dangerous levels of depression and anxiety.

'Many are refusing to go to school, or are about to leave with confidence so low it's hard to see how they can easily move into the world of work and adult relationships,' he says. 'What we want to give them here – why we kick off with that singing session – is a place to rediscover their value to and trust in others.'

They are, ironically, the lucky ones. Not only have these teenagers recognised they need help, but they have families who have sought it out. Bradley knows there are tens of thousands of others who, feeling scared or even ashamed, might not have properly revealed their experience of school bullying to their families. Some have parents who might have been persuaded by the school that the problem is with their child, and who don't know where to turn next. These are the children and young people who can end up leaving school with no friends, no results and no confidence in their future and no idea of the help out there.

'Parents and carers who do call on us know that however much they love their kids, and tell them they love them, they cannot always fight the impact of being unloved by their peers,' he says. 'Not only the bullies but by bystanders who've done nothing to help. It's the latter that often add to that feeling of worthlessness.'

Bullying rears its head over and over in the arena of mental health. It's a complicated piece of the puzzle because of its bi-directional nature. Bullying can be the direct cause of mental health problems, usually when the perpetrators seek out and sabotage a child's schooling because they're distinct in some way. Children who turn to Kidscape usually come bearing differences in the way they learn, in the way they dress, or because of sexuality, ethnicity, religion or disability. Bullying can, quite simply, eat away at a young person's confidence and self-esteem until they're depressed and isolated and more vulnerable to bullying than ever. If it persists, and continually focuses on their difference from the group, it can cause them to hate themselves, and develop a negative self-identity.

But we also know children are often bullied *because* of their mental health issues. They can be struggling with anxiety about family break-up or academic pressure, experiencing social difficulties because of a caring role they've taken on, or suffering depression after trauma or loss. But when those things make them withdrawn, anxious or angry, they are more likely to cause victimisation and social exclusion. Problems might be aggravated if mental health problems have been inadvertently stigmatised at school, or because children struggling haven't had a response to their cry for help, or simply don't know where to turn. It may be their problems have led to their own disruptive behaviour and instigated the wrong kind of response or support.

'What has become evident is that bullying – wherever it starts – has a bigger impact than many schools realise,' says Bradley. Kidscape has plenty of evidence of this, but a study published in *The Lancet Psychiatry*[1] suggests that children who are bullied are at greater risk of mental health problems in later life than those who are maltreated by adults at home – even though the latter

---

1   Lereya, S. T., Copeland, W. E., Costello, E. J. and Wolke, D. 'Adult mental health consequences of peer bullying and maltreatment in childhood: two cohorts in two countries.' *The Lancet Psychiatry (2)*6, pp.524–31.

have been the focus of greater concern in relation to children's mental health. The same report suggested those bullied are five times more likely to experience anxiety and twice as likely to talk of suffering depression and self-harm.

'Given nearly one in three children has been bullied in the last year, and nearly half of children and young people say they've been bullied at some point while at school,[2] this presents heads and their staff with a huge problem but also a great opportunity to promote emotional wellbeing via an anti-bullying policy,' he says.

What you should know about bullying

Bullying is defined as the repetitive, intentional hurting of one person or group by another person or group, where the relationship involves the imbalance of power. It is this 'power issue' that schools are learning to recognise, rather than judging individual incidents on the severity of the injury. In fact, misunderstanding the part the power culture plays has caused teachers to ignore subtler abuse such as teasing or banter, or persistent exclusion from friendship groups when issues spiral out of control. In fact, bullying within 'friendship' groups can be the hardest to spot, in real time or online, says Bradley. From the outside, it can seem like just a group dynamic, but on the inside the victim might feel desperate to stay part of the group and not want to recognise, never mind speak up about, the abusive nature of the relationship. The individual might even become adept at pretending everything is okay while hiding away at breaks or eating their lunch in the loos, and then going back into class unable to engage or concentrate.

2   Anti-Bullying Alliance (2014) *Key Statistics*. Available at www.anti-bullyingalliance.org.uk/research/key-statistics, accessed on 30 August 2016.

Kidscape knows these are all huge things for teachers to get their heads round when they're already trying to do so much for pupils, but they also believe it underlines the crucial role the school can play in promoting healthy relationships and better mental health. 'Schools are uniquely placed to establish a climate of understanding and acceptance in relation to mental health and, when they do, they can reduce the risk of bullying,' says Bradley. Kidscape's training and resources set out how simply listening and hearing and recognising how a pupil is feeling, and offering help – rather than questioning the truth of their accusations or interpretations of events – can be so important. The charity underlines the importance of promoting inclusive behaviour, and championing reporting of bullying to cut through the fear many children feel when they see it going on. And it delivers staff training which can ensure a whole school approach to the issue.

'Schools have, we hope, seen the evidence and shelved any lingering belief that being treated badly at school toughens you up for the "real" world outside it,' says Bradley. 'Most know that bullying doesn't serve any useful purpose at all. But at the same time many don't know how to recognise bullying, what to do about it effectively or have a full understanding of an anti-bullying policy and the crucial difference it can make.'

Kidscape delivers anti-bullying training as part of a teacher's CPD to hundreds of teachers each year, and says that often it can split a single school's staff into nine groups to discuss a bullying scenario and hear nine different opinions about what the child's need was, whether the behaviour towards them was bullying, and how the school should react. 'That is a clear indication of how unfamiliar teachers are with the anti-bullying policy, or how unclear it is,' says Bradley.

What Kidscape want is to establish in its sessions is not only what bullying is but why people bully. There's a line, it says, between building resilience through social interactions and friendships and falling-outs, which are not always easy, versus bullying which is different and dangerous and serves no useful purpose at all. 'Teachers know that a child who feels isolated and unhappy, or whose every interaction in the playground is negative, is simply not going to learn anything useful, either in the moment itself or when they get back into class.

'But our training also helps them see that bullying is often hidden from teachers by both bully and victim, and part of our job is to help school staff pick up on the signs and symptoms earlier, so they can act in response,' he says.

'One of the first things we ask teachers to think about is the culture of the school. Too often we hear about a culture of leaders and followers, or populars and unpopulars. It's that imbalance – and a culture that feeds it – which can allow bullying to thrive and where bystanders are encouraged to stay silent.'

Teachers who work with Kidscape often come to recognise that children who appear confident, popular and even leaders, have apparently crossed the line into the area where they are manipulative and aggressive and controlling, explains Bradley. 'They might have loads of friends and appear happy as a result, but schools are doing them no favours by ignoring their oppressive behaviour.' He explains how they can easily become bullies, demanding loyalty from the group who, in turn, become effective bystanders, watching nervously as others are picked on and learning that they have no power to change things. 'We hear this story over and over from children who call on us or come to the workshops. They might have recognised the bully has real problems, and is even disliked by others; but they can't understand why those others, sometimes children they consider friends, do nothing. That's like the final straw.'

Kidscape aims to help teachers understand that ignoring these dynamics doesn't help the bully, the bystander or the child being bullied. 'Children who bully might say the right things in class or in an assembly, but they have to show they have learned it in the way they behave outside the class, and teachers have to continue the learning there. It's crucial in helping these children find their place in society,' says Bradley.

With this in mind, he refers to another initiative Kidscape has developed which aims, it hopes, to make a bigger change, and reduce demand for the kind of workshops families turn to when things have got beyond bad. While Bradley is with the teenagers at the residential workshop, other members of his team are at Oliver Goldsmith Primary School in South London where a group of teachers are experiencing BIT (Bullying Intervention Training). This is a part-government funded project which takes Kidscape's expertise into primary schools to reach years 4 and 5 – the age bullying often starts to rear its head. It's designed to equip teachers and pupils with the skills they need to understand and prevent the problem.

'We all think we know what a bully is, but there was a lack of understanding in our team about how it starts, and who is vulnerable,' says Tracy Brook, safeguarding and special needs coordinator at the school. 'Kidscape's training in classes, with parents/carers and with teaching teams, is helping us unpick that. I think some of the teachers recognised that they'd felt intimidated by tackling the emotional stuff, and the tremendous pressure from the curriculum doesn't help. But they came out of the sessions better equipped to understand the symptoms of bullying and how to tackle it more quickly. They came out feeling really positive about strategies – relevant to their everyday experience – to take into class.'

But one of the most powerful lessons they're learning is about school culture. 'We are recognising how children might take on ideas from lessons or assemblies that promote understanding and then talk the talk. But teaching has to show them how to live the lesson,' says Brook. 'We've all seen how children – perhaps the more vulnerable or lacking in confidence – can be desperate for approval from the strong characters in the class. We have, via this training, sought to introduce ideas to encourage those who have leadership skills to use them in a positive rather than a negative way.

'We're a "telling" school that champions children to speak up when they see something which they know is wrong, and we promote emotional wellbeing – we have a team of therapists and have run mindfulness and mentoring projects here. But anti-bullying strategies have to be part of the picture if children are to benefit from all or any of the other initiatives. If children are not happy and secure they won't be ready to learn anything, no matter how much you throw at them.'

At the time of writing, 250 schools and 20,000 children have benefited from Kidscape Bullying Intervention Training in primary schools. Independent research shows that 98 per cent of professionals felt more confident about preventing bullying as a result, while some 92 per cent of children said they realised how bullying affects people and 84 per cent felt more confident and better about themselves. Crucially 93 per cent of schools that have had the training reported a decrease in bullying behaviour.

'The research is showing us that bullying is not an inevitable part of school life and that interventions can play a crucial part in behaviour and children's emotional wellbeing,' says Bradley. 'If we can reach them at this young age, and give them the confidence and skills they need, we believe that can have an enormous impact as they move into secondary education.

'A school where everyone feels valued – where you have a more equable balance of power, and where it's normal and natural for children to help each other – benefits everyone, including the bullies and the bystanders,' says Bradley. 'When schools address bullying and introduce schemes that harness all the good in children – say via peer mentoring, playground buddy schemes, lunchtime clubs or social action initiatives – schools are seeing that children, far from inevitably bullying each other, form new kinds of connections which enrich the life and enhance the education of everyone, every day.'

Kidscape offers a range of bespoke courses for teachers, parents and children, which can be adapted to suit your needs or setting and cover everything from assertiveness skills for children, to reviews of anti-bullying policies for head teachers. Protecting children from harm is a legal requirement for schools and relies on staff being properly trained, aware of and able to apply the school's anti-bullying policy. If you'd like to find out more about how the charity could help your school visit www.kidscape.org.uk.

In My View

Gok Wan on creating a kinder culture in schools

Gok Wan is an author, award-winning TV presenter and fashion expert. In his autobiography *Through Thick and Thin* he talks candidly about his experience of being bullied at school, and what happened next. He is now an ambassador for the anti-bullying charity Kidscape.

Attitudes to mental health are changing in society and there is a new conversation going on – we're seeing more written about mental health, more high profile figures talking about mental health, and there's more understanding about the impact bullying can have on mental health. But that shouldn't make people feel they don't have to worry any more. That we're all fine and all good to go. We're really not. There is a lot more to say, and to do.

I was bullied at school – it was insidious and clever, a constant drip drip of insults and sneers and name calling. The teachers did nothing to help – they walked the other way. I felt isolated and terribly lonely. I was lucky to come through it and see it was not my fault, and I learned the hard way the real power of kindness. It has shaped the way I work since. But I know when you're going through this it feels enormous, the most awful thing, and for some the effects can be lasting and devastating.

There will, of course, always be bullies, but there has to be a better way to help children facing bullying right now to understand that it is not their fault, and the way they feel – the anxiety and depression and loneliness – is nothing to be ashamed of, and something they can talk about. That's where Kidscape is brilliant. Its workshops give those children a voice and a sense of community, and help them see they're not alone. Kidscape has also brought a conversation about bullying and mental health into schools. It doesn't shy away from the difficult questions about why children bully and it doesn't make anyone the victim. It knows both the bullies and the bullied need support. Children bully because they're unhappy, or because they've been bullied themselves or are facing really horrible stuff at home. They need support, too, so they can find a different way of expressing their frustrations and sadness.

This is where a kinder, more equitable school culture can help. Kidscape knows that if the culture is unfair, unequal and unsupportive it doesn't help anyone. Changing it is a huge and difficult challenge, not least because while we can teach children how to treat each other better, the adults around them might be behaving in a different way. Not just the adults they know, but the adults they see on TV – who are sometimes put on a pedestal. Look at the way comedians on stage get laughs at others' expense, or the way the media can treat people, or the way politicians shout and scowl and are vile to each other. This is all on the six o'clock news for kids to see.

We need to think about how, against that backdrop, we can create a fairer, kinder culture, and teach children the difference between right and wrong; teach them the difference between a joke and the kind of banter and language that is bullying and harmful; teach them that we can all feel vulnerable but, at the same time, we can all support each other, and that we will all be heard. Then, maybe, children can help adults make a change for the better.

6

The Counsellor

Discovering the Power of a Place to Talk, and to Be Heard and Understood

School-based counsellors can not only help children cope with life's struggles, they can help them learn and grow, says the charity Place2Be. They introduced us to one of the scores of schools where they work to see the difference it can make.

'It's too easy for schools like ours to search for and focus on the cause of behaviour, a diagnosis that might explain it, or even for someone else to blame when things aren't going well in the classroom. Now we know we should look for more immediate solutions.'
YVONNE WOZNIAK, HEAD TEACHER, ST JOSEPH'S

In a small room tucked between two classes at St Joseph's Catholic Primary School in Putney, South London, the walls are lined with a doll's house, a mini sandpit, a small table and four tiny chairs. Shelves along one side are stacked with soft toys, paint and a glorious array of coloured glitter. A row of cardboard boxes, decorated with stick-on jewels and bearing felt-tipped names, are projects in progress. The treasures each box owner makes in their weekly sessions here are stored away in these homemade chests, ready to be taken home when counselling is over.

What is really made in this room, though, is more lasting and life changing. This is Place2Be, one of over 250 revolutionary spaces in the same number of Britain's primary and secondary schools bringing counselling to the classroom and, in particular, to children who need to untangle the weightiest emotional difficulties that might be getting in the way of their learning, friendships and future.

It's here that Place2Be's specially trained counsellors meet with children on a one-to-one basis during lesson time to draw, paint, play and talk. During breaks and lunchtime the room is opened up as a Place2Talk, where groups of children can come and chat about what's on their mind. Throughout the term there are group sessions here for pupils needing help with issues such as bereavement or bullying, self-esteem or a move on to secondary school.

'All life's problems can come into the classroom with the children,' says St Joseph's head teacher, Yvonne Wozniak. 'Place2Be and the counselling it provides is independent of St Joseph's but it's now part of the fabric of our school. The counsellors share our mission to help each child learn, and it's our belief that unless they are happy they can't learn effectively.'

Place2Be is a national children's mental health charity providing school-based support across the UK. It launched in 1994, in recognition that thousands of vulnerable children take all sorts of worries into school. Children who, despite their own best efforts to sit and listen, can end up instead consumed by everything that is going on outside the classroom. Last year alone they delivered more than 65,000 one-to-one counselling sessions (some 300 of them at St Joseph's), while over 30,000 children self-referred to Place2Talk to work through issues that were upsetting them.

This charity's power for good (now championed by their royal patron, HRH The Duchess of Cambridge) is now proven – research shows that 73 per cent of the children they reach who have severe difficulties improve after counselling, 62 per cent improve in their learning, and 79 per cent say friendships are better. This is not only down to its being right where kids are each day, and right when they need it, it's also as a result of the meticulously planned, multilayered service. The counsellors are supported on a daily basis by a core Place2Be team who provide not just clinical supervision but bespoke expert advice (for example, on special needs or a safeguarding issue) and, where needed, signposts to relevant outside agencies local to the school.

Yvonne Wozniak acknowledges that before Place2Be came on the scene she was, as the school's head teacher, looking for ways to better support children who were sent out of class and into her office because of their behaviour.

'Children come here with diverse and complex needs,' she explains. 'The leafy suburban streets of Putney belie the issues our families face. Nearly one in ten pupils have special educational needs and disabilities, nearly one in three are from families who are disadvantaged, and more than one in seven are from ethnic minority families, which can create language and cultural issues. Most families live in social housing on the outskirts of this area. Many travel an hour to get here and some, for example those from the local women's refuge, are just here for a few weeks or months.'

Regardless of how long or short their stay is, and regardless of their background, they are all treated as an essential part of the school community. 'We believe if we build the right relationship with them – a relationship based on trust, value and reciprocated respect – we can teach them anything,' says Wozniak. 'We turned to Place2Be as a reaction to the challenges the school was facing, unsure of the solutions.'

The project that emerged has, it's clear, proved to be proactive rather than reactive, identifying and meeting needs quickly and effectively. The school's pupil referrals to CAMHS are now rare.

'We've learned as a result that it's too easy for schools like ours to search for and focus on the cause of behaviour, a diagnosis that might explain it, or even for someone else to blame when things aren't going well in the classroom. Now we know we should look for more immediate solutions that will make those same children feel better more quickly and so be more able to make friends, to take part in school life, and to learn and progress.'

Part of the school team

Place2Be's Liz Booker is St Joseph's lead counsellor. She's been working at the school for four years and is considered an independent but integral part of the school team; a feature at the gate each morning as she chats and liaises with parents, a regular presence in assemblies and at staff, SENCO (special education needs coordinator) and new parent meetings. She manages a specially trained team of volunteer counsellors who help deliver the one-to-one sessions (for children referred by parents and/or teachers) and leads the Place2Talk at break and lunch (where children can self-refer), and now a Place2Think for teachers (more of which below).

'I think as adults, and as teachers, we tend to think children are naturally resilient and perhaps not badly affected by parents breaking up or dealing with addiction or debt, or grandparents dying, or siblings struggling with their health,' says Booker. 'Kids are indeed extraordinarily resilient, but they need help to build that. With the right support they can learn to negotiate their feelings and build skills to help them cope throughout their life, including the skill to ask for help when they need it.'

Space to be quiet, and to speak volumes

There is a reason St Joseph's Place2Be room is stuffed full of toys and art materials for these sessions, explains Sarah Kendrick, Place2Be's head of service in the south of England. 'Schools are very focused on words and speaking and listening, but children's means of expression often isn't verbal. For the first few years of their life they communicate in non-verbal ways, and we feel it's good to get back to that.'

Kendrick explains children are often identified as needing help, not because of what they say but because of how they behave – perhaps they've been disruptive in class, aggressive in the playground or withdrawn from their peer group. 'They can't always explain why in a few words in a few minutes with a teacher,' she says. 'In a relationship with the counsellor they benefit from expressing their feelings through play or art, and that can help them work through things going on in their life. The counsellor has the time and space to let them do that and children welcome the opportunity; we see that overwhelmingly.'

One of the clear benefits of the programme is the way it helps the school act quickly when it senses children are struggling – their behaviour might be discussed at a meeting with the head teacher, SENCO, parent or carer, educational psychologist (on site once a week) and Liz Booker. Counselling can start soon after, and can then run for many months, without taking children out of school.

Place2Be knows, too, that all children – not only those referred to counselling – benefit as a result. Not only from classes without distractions (around 75 per cent of children who go to counselling are less disruptive as a result), but crucially by an atmosphere in the school that prioritises emotional wellbeing.

'We have built something special here,' says Booker. 'A culture where children are taking responsibility for their own and others' wellbeing.' She believes the project is helping children recognise it's natural to talk about their feelings and worries, right to ask for help when they are struggling. 'It was a slow build, not an overnight transformation,' she says. 'But now the children might talk about anything: how they're missing their dad since he left, or their worry about a poorly relative, or why they're feeling lonely and left out in the playground, or how bad they feel about not being any good at football. If it's bothering them, it helps to talk about it. No problem is too small. It is a complete privilege to help them feel listened to, valued and validated.'

Giving parents and teachers their place to be

Parents and carers are a key part of this. They do, of course, have to give consent for one-to-one counselling but, at the same time, it's hugely beneficial for parents and carers to engage in and understand the psychological life of their child. 'When a parent or teacher better understands the behaviour of a child, even a subtle change in their stance on it can bring enormous change in the quality of the relationship,' says Kendrick.

It was the vital part parents and carers play in both the learning and wellbeing of children that led the charity to launch what they call Place for Parents – which can include counselling for up to a year with a specially trained parent counsellor. There are also socials and coffee mornings where families can meet to hear more about the service in school and other relevant mental health services outside it. Those parents in turn become champions of the service. Some 74 per cent say things improve at home as a result of Place2Be's work with their children.

Schools like St Joseph's are also offered a Place2Think, one of the charity's newer services to support teachers' own mental health. This is increasingly recognised as crucial if they are to support children in their class.

'Unlike other professionals in the social care sector, teachers don't have therapeutic supervision, an obvious place to take their own anxieties or an obvious person to hold them,' says Kendrick. 'Place2Be offers training for teachers – including special training for those who are newly qualified or coming to the profession via schemes like Teach First – and the service called Place2Think.' As the name suggests, this is a place for teachers to take a breath, and to talk about and better understand the behaviour they are seeing and the children who concern them and – within a therapeutic framework – support each other.

'Once teachers realise the counsellor they're talking with can contain and hold their anxieties, fears and concerns about children, they continue to bring issues to them,' she says. 'It becomes a supervisory consultancy relationship. The more they use the service, the more easily teachers are able to discuss their anxieties more openly, and support each other more effectively.

'Relationships underpin everything humans do from the moment we're born. Everyone needs to be treated with respect and given time and attention,' adds Kendrick. 'Our feeling is that, no matter where a child has come from and the troubles they have, they'll benefit from a school replicating positive attachment and a reliable parenting style. We want to form those positive relationships with parents, teachers and children in each school, and help them go on to form relationships on that basis with each other.'

A case for change

Despite evidence showing how this kind of specialist counselling can play a massively positive part in promoting children's mental health and wellbeing, a recent survey suggested that only a third of the country's primary schools have a counsellor on site. Of these, the majority (nearly six out of ten) are only at the school one day a week or less; and schools aren't always sure what clinical supervision and support they have.

Most head teachers would like this to change and in primary settings across the country have raised pupil wellbeing and mental health as one of their top concerns. Financial constraints and a lack of qualified local professionals are cited as the key barriers to progress, with time constraints and a lack of relationship with social care also appearing on the problem list.

Place2Be counsellors like Liz Booker and models like the one at Putney are largely funded by the schools themselves, but the service is also supported by corporate sponsors and charitable donations. The charity's own independent economic analysis[1] has found that every pound spent on this early intervention creates a return of £6 in terms of savings to society. Place2Be is now aiming to be part of dozens more schools by the year 2020 and is doing outreach work – training mental health champions to work in schools who don't benefit from its full model.

'Teachers are doing a brilliant job, looking after up to 30 children at any one time and with the opportunity to have a positive influence on each one's mental health,' says Kendrick. 'But that's a huge ask when you look at some of the issues those 30 children bring into school, and the work teachers have to do to meet so many targets.'

'St Joseph's is an emotionally literate school and Yvonne had the emotional lives of children at the heart of her thinking before we arrived,' says Kendrick. 'But schools where we work, however sceptical at the start, all open up to the idea of counselling when they feel the benefits. The focus of their attention shifts, and then the teams start to look at other ideas to support their pupil's mental health and emotional wellbeing, too.'

---

1   The Place2Be (2010) *Cost Effective Positive Outcomes for Children and Families: An Economic Analysis of The Place2Be's Integrated School-Based Services for Children.* London: ThePlace2Be.

'All teachers want to help children, but we know many can bring their own parenting and teaching style to a post,' says Wozniak who, despite Place2Be, still has an office littered with toys and an open door for any child who needs a breather and a safe place to hang out. 'I know some of our own teaching and support staff might have grappled with our approach to start with, but I think crucial to any teaching is the skill to recognise what you don't know, and what you can learn from others.

'Working as a team with Place2Be has changed this school,' she adds. 'When we recruit new teachers they know from the outset the way we work, our ethos that puts children at the centre of what we do, and has their happiness as the top priority. No one ever complains about a child leaving their class for counselling. It might take some time for them to see the benefits, but they do. They always do.'

Place2Be was launched by Dame Benita Refson, whose work counselling adolescents and her understanding of the need to reach and support children with problems earlier in their lives inspired her to set up an independent charity called The Place to Be in 1994, which later became Place2Be in 2012. Refson has seen the organisation grow from five schools to over 250. She has also been behind the development of its support for professionals via specialist training. St Joseph's – the school featured in this chapter – benefits from Place2Be's full model of support, but the charity offers a flexible menu of services and training. If you'd like to find out how they could support your school visit www.place2be.org.uk.

In My View

Professor Tanya Byron on the vital role of early interventions

Broadcaster, author and clinical psychologist Professor Tanya Byron is an ambassador for Place2Be.

Children who are withdrawn and non-communicative, isolating themselves from normal life, or angry and aggressive to themselves or others, often cannot find the words to express their overwhelming anxiety and unhappiness. Self-harm, restricted eating, school refusal, antisocial behaviour are examples of behaviours displayed by unhappy children.

Teachers are not always equipped to deal with the problems they see. They don't have mandatory mental health training and they work in places often driven by targets and testing. When they pick up pupils struggling with really serious issues they can, too often, feel unable to meet their needs and find there is nowhere for them to go for help, even though they know the earlier the intervention the more likely they can help prevent more acute mental health issues. Teachers may be amazing educators but they often feel powerless. They know the waiting list for CAMHS is long and the threshold for accessing help high.

We know that more than half of all adults with mental health problems were diagnosed in childhood, yet less than half were treated appropriately at the time. We must, as a compassionate society, provide all possible resources to schools so they can intervene early with evidence-based assessment and treatment.

This is where projects like Place2Be can help. There is, at last, a growing awareness that emotional intelligence and resilience are fundamental aspects of healthy child development and play a vital role in helping children develop into successful adults. I'd like to see projects like Place2Be become part and parcel of the education system, part of what schools do. They offer a space for children to think through not just mental health issues, but developmental issues, and a place to think them through with someone who is trained and who has the time to support them. I think that space embedded in a school as it is at St Joseph's gives everyone a more holistic perspective on what education means and what education can do.

7

The Conversation

Transforming the Relationship
Between School and Family, and
the Emotional Wellbeing of the
Pupil They Both Want to Help

In schools across the land, parents and carers can
be seen as part of the problem when pupils are
struggling. They should, instead, be seen as part of
the solution, says the charity Achievement for All. They
took us to a school in Oldham to show us how.

'We want teachers to recognise they don't need to know it
all and never will know it all, and that a crucial part of their
job and pedagogical practice is learning something new from
each other and from pupils and their families every day...'

PROFESSOR SONIA BLANDFORD,
CEO ACHIEVEMENT FOR ALL

In the hubbub of conversation and laughter, a group of parents
are passing round bacon sandwiches and mugs of tea. Sarnies
served, they fall back on the sofas chatting about their week,

glad to put their feet up after the morning dash to get their children into school. One is explaining how she's just signed up for a learning group at the local college to get the literacy and numeracy qualifications she needs for work, which she reckons will also help her son with his homework. Another talks about her own daughter and some of the struggles she has in class, but how far she's come this term. They discuss school trips, class events, and about a new learning initiative in year 5. Two women are bent over school laptops on a table nearby, sorting out a housing problem, they say.

This is Stoneleigh Academy, a primary school in Oldham, and as the parents chat, they're joined by Rachael Finn, Assistant Head, just out of assembly. Two parents on a sofa shuffle up to make room, while another goes to put the kettle on. Not only because a cup of tea is what every teacher needs on a Friday morning, but because this meeting of minds – parents and teachers together – is helping bring something special and significant to Stoneleigh that has helped transform the school. The parents here are not members of the PTA, or any of the usual suspects schools come to expect to be hanging around wanting to help. The parents here were, the school say, the hardest to reach and the least involved. Some were seriously suspicious of schools (thanks to their experience as pupils), others seriously overwhelmed by issues at home and many were seriously unhappy because they felt their kids were not thriving in class the way they should. Until now, that is.

Stoneleigh Academy is based in an area of the North West facing some of the most serious social and economic problems. Rachael Finn, acting head of Stoneleigh, says when children arrive in reception 95 per cent are way below the base line and are often from families with huge challenges (long-term unemployment, housing crises, health problems).

'We understood those parents' aspirations might have been destroyed, and that can damage their aspirations for their children, too,' says Finn. 'We wanted to change that. We want the children here to move to secondary not only having achieved beyond expectations, but with a sense of their own worth and a belief in their own future. You can't do that with children in isolation. We realised you have to work with parents and carers too, to understand how to reach their children more effectively.'

Of course no school intends to alienate parents. In fact, most include a mission statement promoting the relationship they want to have with families, and many – when asked about this issue – pride themselves on the numbers who turn up to parents' evenings or the funds those parents raise for school projects.

But the nature of school inevitably exposes the fault lines. The children who are late, always without their PE kit, failing to deliver homework, unable to focus in class, kicking off in the playground or finding it hard to mix with others – they all trigger worries in schools about what issues their pupils are bringing in from home. The inevitable resultant problems at school (discipline, friendship issues, learning problems, anxieties) then create further worries for families about what is happening at school. And in the meantime, communication lines can crumble.

What reconnected the two sides and triggered this transformation at Stoneleigh was a new kind of conversation between parent and teacher. Dozens of conversations actually, and they were, say Stoneleigh, pivotal in driving change and the start of something really exciting.

Raising aspirations by giving parents a voice

The 'conversations' were introduced by the charity Achievement for All, which aims to raise the achievement and aspirations for the 'bottom' 20 per cent of every school, and by doing that, promote their confidence and build their self-worth. In recent years,

Achievement for All has become a guiding force in thousands of schools across the UK, bringing a whole raft of ideas, resources, professional development training and network opportunities to the table – via specially trained coaches who support school improvement. But it is pupils' families, and in particular what they call 'structured conversations' they use to engage with and learn from them, that the charity say are central to their success story, and to the staggering improvement in results at the schools where they work.

'Like it or not, any disconnect between parents and teachers can lead to judgements on both sides,' says Achievement for All's founder and CEO, Professor Sonia Blandford. 'When you mend that relationship something wonderful can happen.'

It has, according to Blandford, never been so important. Not only does she recognise the contradiction in what is said by the government about prioritising mental health and what's actually being done in schools, she sees the same incongruity in the attitude to parents. On the one hand, policy and research recognise their crucial role; but on the other, initiatives are introduced that appear to alienate or even demonise them.

'I think while most leadership teams want good relationships with their parents, and know it has an impact on outcomes and attendance, we're at a time when an "us and them" atmosphere is growing,' she says, citing media stories about parents being banned from school grounds unless they have an appointment, being told what they can and can't wear at the school gate, or being taken to court for taking a family holiday out of term time. And she mentions coverage of policies indicating parents might no longer be 'compulsory' on school governing boards – professionals with the 'right skills' being favoured instead.

'None of these things suggest that schools fully recognise the vital role of parents in informing a child's learning and yet all the research shows how important it is. Research by Professor Charles Desforges at Exeter University, for example, reveals the important fact that parents have a greater influence on a child's learning than teachers. A partnership between the two, therefore, is the only practical way forward.'

Blandford – who continues to be listed in Debrett's 100 Most Influential for her work in schools – believes parents are one of the most under-explored but powerful drivers of emotional wellbeing in every school.

'We know that all children, including those from the most challenging home environments, want love and respect from their family. It's the stuff that builds their inner cores and their self-efficacy, and if that doesn't grow it can lead to all sorts of inner conflicts which manifest in the classroom,' she says. 'Instead of blaming home for that, schools have an opportunity to engage with families and carers in a way that helps the child feel valued, by both parties.' For Achievement for All, this isn't about trying to change parents, it's about changing the relationship. It means, says Blandford, 'getting rid of any conflict while supporting parents, and letting them support learning. Even if parents are part of the problem, they are first and foremost partners in raising and educating the child.'

When Achievement for All arrive at a school (and they've worked in over 4500 to date), these structured conversations kick off the whole process. Training in them is crucial and extensive, giving teaching staff skills in coaching and counselling, mentoring and how to meet with parents in a new way that changes the relationship.

'It goes way further than a parent evening or even a one-to-one chat at a parent surgery,' explains Blandford. 'Schools initially have a target group – usually that 20 per cent who are struggling at the bottom. And it allows their parents to listen to the concerns of teachers but – much more importantly – allows teachers to listen to the parents.' The charity says some 80 per cent of schools it works in say the training has completely changed the way they engage with parents and that they often extend the idea beyond the target group, and engage with all parents in a whole new way.

'What prompts people to make rash judgements about each other – parents about teachers or teachers about parents – is their own lack of resilience,' says Blandford. 'If a teacher makes a judgement about parents and their child without all the relevant information and without the skills to really listen, the needs of the child can get lost along the way. The same happens when a parent has a negative experience of the school. They make a judgement, stop attending meetings and socials, and the needs of the child can get lost. What binds these two parties is the commonality of the child, and our aim is to build the resilience of that child by building the resilience of the teacher and the parent. We have found – without exception – that the structured conversation does that, and with marvellous effect.'

Raising outcomes by supporting teachers

Blandford knows this must involve teachers coming to the table to recognise what all good teachers have to recognise – 'that they don't need to know it all and never will know it all, and that a crucial part of their job and pedagogical practice is learning something new from each other and from pupils and their families every day'.

Experience of a 'similar' child with a 'similar' issue can help in those conversations, but it simply isn't enough to inform what they have to do next, she says.

'Teachers need to feel valued by everyone they encounter, just as their pupils do. And teachers are doing so much work, in and out of school, and are in this profession to make a difference. We don't question that,' she says. 'When we go into schools we question what prevents that happening. What is stopping them enjoying their job, learning from each other, collaborating effectively with parents, and getting the best out of their pupils?'

Blandford says structured conversations help answer this question. She says they enable teachers to really *hear* families, and to learn more about the pupils they are trying to reach – their interests and hobbies, fears and dislikes, friendships and foibles, what they like and don't like about school. What a good day looks like and what a bad day looks like and the impact it has.

'This gives the teacher a real opportunity to discover what works for the child and what they can build into the learning,' she says. 'We also know – because families tell us – that parents and carers feel valued and listened to and so able to talk about the barriers to learning they see, for example, a child's caring role, or work, social or health problems at home. It helps schools create a picture of that child's life and needs, which is never used to judge the family or explain away underachievement, but instead used to understand each child and to open up more support to help the pupil. It also gives the teacher a chance to agree learning targets with the family so they can support those targets at home,' she says. When that happens, Blandford says, schools start to see real change – not only in children's results but also in their engagement with and enjoyment of school. As that happens, confidence and self-worth grows too.

'There was definitely a history of negative relationships here,' says Rachael Finn at Stoneleigh. 'Some parents had become frustrated and relationships had broken down so we had to work hard to explain the change we wanted to see when we started working with Achievement for All – organising home visits, coffee mornings and more. I think for some of our parents and carers the idea of extra conversations with teachers was greeted in the same way as an invitation to take extra trips to the dentist. We had to help them see that there would be none of the formality of a parents' evening and that they'd be in control of the conversation. It was all about them. We had to show them we acknowledged that there is more to their child than how they do at school. That we wanted them – the families – to help us help their children.'

Once the structured conversations got underway Finn says a new mood was set and the relationship changed into something really positive, and helped them change everything else too.

'Parents could talk about what was and wasn't working for their children, and what help they needed at home. We suddenly had an insight into the children's home life and as parents opened up we could see how much more we had to learn, and how much more we could and should engage. In this new atmosphere of openness and trust, Finn says, they were also able to show parents how the school wanted to help them, too, with everything from debt problems to housing issues. 'They can use the phones or computers here, or we can signpost agencies who offer assistance,' she explains.

'We can see how well that works – if we have a positive impact on our pupil's home life, and if we listen to parents and learn from them about what their child needs, there is always a positive impact on the child,' she says. That, in turn, led to more ideas – like the Friday morning get-togethers and a new parent representative group led by parents who hadn't been involved before and who provide a bridge between home and school to others like them.

'In fact parents who hadn't engaged at all with the school in the past now want to be really involved, and to help their children get on. You can see and hear how engaged and supportive they are from those sharing breakfast with us on a Friday morning.'

Stoneleigh Academy, once a struggling school, is now listed as one of the top 100 primary schools in England and the leadership and management of the school has been rated by Ofsted as outstanding.

'It's not a magic bullet, but it is magical to watch,' says Sonia Blandford. 'When children feel understood and valued their confidence grows, and this impacts on everything from their learning to their friendships.'

Blandford has a bounty of stories that stem from conversations with home, and from ideas parents have brought to the table – from whole school mentoring programmes (see pp.19–26) to new kinds of lunchtime clubs. She talks about the teenager who landed at his fifth school suffering acute anxieties but who, as a result of a structured conversation, was taken under the wing of a teacher who shared his passion for computers; a school refuser being mentored by a caretaker to harness his love of gardening (using seeds and bedding plants to practise maths and to give him confidence at the start of each day); and the parent who was taught to read by his child's school so he could help his daughter progress. Schools like Stoneleigh have told her how the simplest things, like hearing about and harnessing a child's passion (for motorbikes or trucks or space or dance) can be the key to helping a child feel recognised and understood and so more engaged in school life.

'It's the individual initiatives that come out of these conversations that continue to amaze me,' she says. 'The benefits are greater than the sum of all the stories I could tell you but they matter so much because they represent a child who is better understood, and so better supported and able to learn. Teachers may initially feel they have no time or room for this kind of thing, but when they see the transformation there really is no going back.'

Achievement for All is a national charity supporting thousands of schools who want to make a difference to children and teenagers, including those vulnerable to underachievement. When the charity goes into a school they establish an initial needs analysis and identify the target group, usually around 20 per cent of pupils. Then – via coaching and staff development, including training in the structured conversations that kick off the process – they help schools create and implement a programme plan and develop teaching and learning strategies to increase opportunities for the target group. Coaching support continues via INSET days and bi-weekly visits from an appointed coach for two years, and schools have access to a wealth of resources (via the charity's online learning hub called The Bubble) and are integrated into an overlapping set of communities of practice via thousands of other schools. To find out more about what they could offer you visit www.afaeducation.org.

8

The Role Model

Introducing Your Pupils to a Powerful New Kind of Educator

Hundreds of role models up and down the land
are hoping their experience can help children
and teenagers shape a better, healthier future. We
went to meet some working in schools today.

'In every school there is this sense of a load being lifted and
fears assuaged. The students know in that session they're in an
environment where they can ask questions. There are no silly
questions ever. This starts a conversation where they can talk
about anything...'

SARA PRESTON, BEAT

If you think you're too small to make a difference, try going
to bed with a mosquito in the room, quipped the late Anita
Roddick in one of her many bids to spark social action and
activism. Her words might come to mind today as, around the
country, young people, not much older, bolder or even bigger
than the pupils they are visiting, march into classrooms around
the UK to share their tales: stories of eating disorders and self-

harm; of homophobic terror in the playground; of being a British Muslim in an emerging multicultural community and of defying expectations for what their future could hold. And as they talk – think pins dropping in the classrooms they're in today – pupils are looking up and listening and learning something about the world, and about themselves.

The power of a role model is well established – it's often been called the most powerful form of educating in and out of school. But this isn't about hauling in an ad hoc ex-student or guest speaker for a ten-minute pep talk. The role models we're meeting today are in school to give their audience lessons in self-awareness and self-confidence, on occasions bringing issues to life that teachers can either fear or feel ill equipped to talk about, worried it might make things worse rather than better. To be effective in the classroom their work is put in context (teachers are prepped in advance and supported via workshops or e-learning), are anonymous (better to avoid using an old pupil who students might already have a view on) and are meticulously trained by the charities they represent.

They're also turning on its head what a role model can be, too. At a time when young people are, with the help of social media, perpetually comparing themselves to and trying to emulate others (too often 'others' who provide a distorted view of what the student should be doing or wanting for their own personal gain), these role models talk about the differences or challenges they share with their young peers; and they're doing it all for free. What's more, rather than saying 'follow in my footsteps and be like me', they're helping young people discover something wonderful about themselves so they can be true to that. As a result, they can better look after their health, or stand up for their beliefs, or seek out a future that uses their talents and potential to make their own kind of change.

Me and my anorexia: role models working to beat eating disorders

Chelsea Rocks is a beautiful, bubbly 19-year-old. She's telling the teenagers in front of her in this classroom in Edinburgh how she missed her prom, a summer with her pals and a whole load of teenage things she wished she hadn't missed as the result of an eating disorder. 'I felt I was overweight,' she says. 'I felt other people had noticed, and I was desperate to fit in. I was trying to look the best I could for everyone else in a bid to please everyone else. But instead of fitting in I alienated myself. Pretty soon I was avoiding friends, embarrassed by what I was doing to myself but not knowing how to stop. In the end I left school for a while. I was risking my health. In fact it was when I was risking my chance of ever having children that I started my recovery.'

The children in the room have heard about eating disorders in a recent PSHE session, and some may know of peers already struggling. But teachers know that meeting someone their age, someone they'd like to be (Chelsea is studying politics and social policy at university, already has a job and projects an aura of someone with the world at her feet, even while she has her feet on the ground) feels totally different from being told something by a member of staff.

'I am just speaking to them about me at school,' Rocks says later. 'They're my peers, and right now are the age I was when I was affected. I'm shocked now by the need I felt to be older before my time. The need to keep up and fit in by being like others instead of being myself. In every classroom I go into you can see they understand that and are paying attention.'

Rocks says when she talks about the things young people do because they think everyone else rates them ('have a girl or boyfriend, look like a supermodel, try stuff we shouldn't try') she can sense their relief when she reveals that other teenagers often don't rate them at all, but are just trying to keep up too. 'I don't tell them not to wear makeup or dismiss the desire to look nice,' she says. 'I just want to help them think about *why* they do what they do. When I talk about the need to slow down and enjoy these years you can see they get that, and want it too.'

Chelsea Rocks is a specially trained young ambassador for Beat, the UK's eating disorder charity. She's one of 26 in Scotland and part of a large national team. This charity works to support the thousands experiencing this mental health condition – at the last count there were 725,000 men and women diagnosed with an eating disorder, with girls aged 12–20 at high risk. Anorexia nervosa has the highest mortality rate of all psychiatric illnesses. One in five sufferers die early as a result of the physical consequences or suicide.

The charity recruits carefully, meeting each role model and exploring their experience and recovery via meetings and group work so it can be sure the team have enough critical distance from their own experience for their own sake and for those they'll be speaking to. Many, like Chelsea, are teenagers themselves. They're supervised and supported through their early visits and each school receives resources so they can build on the session in subsequent PSHE classes. Beat knows that while there is a commonality in their ambassadors' illnesses, they may represent the million different experiences of the condition. That includes the contributing factors, the way the illness impacted on their life, education, friends and family, the turning point that caused them to seek help (some positive, some negative) and what eventually went on to enable them to get better. Where possible, they try to have a few young ambassadors going into a school rather than just one, but individuals like Chelsea – here on her own today – demonstrate an astounding maturity and ability to reflect. She talks about the plethora of experiences, with anorexia and bulimia and other forms of self-harm, and is able to challenge myths and misconceptions as she answers questions, many outside her own personal experience. Her training has also included the rules of engagement. No details are given about how she (or anyone else) lost weight, details that might be used in the wrong way by others who are struggling.

Beat's Young People's Project Officer for Scotland, Sara Preston, says they know from their research that many school staff have had little or no training in this issue, and many say they are afraid to talk about issues like eating disorders or self-harm for fear of triggering problems in pupils or complaints from parents. 'But it is so important to open a conversation like this. All the feedback we get – from clinicians and teachers – demonstrates it's as powerful as the theoretical knowledge they can deliver,' she says. 'We know that teachers are under huge pressure and can get a hard rap. We know that the ones we meet would go to every CPD training course on offer if there was the time and the money. We hope we're not only empowering pupils but empowering teachers by working with them, so they can learn more about these issues.' The charity not only covers the more well-known physical symptoms but the psychological, emotional and behavioural signs often overlooked in the early stages.

Preston reckons that one of the many things ambassadors do so well is helping young people feel they are not alone. By sharing the journey they've been on, and how they found help and came out the other side, she believes they can make young people feel less isolated. 'In every school there is this sense of a load being lifted and fears assuaged. The students know in that session they're in an environment where they can ask questions. There are no silly questions ever. This starts a conversation where they can talk about anything.'

What I did next: the Muslim role models raising the bar

It is a new kind of conversation that brings a group of young Muslims to a secondary school in Birmingham on a wet Wednesday morning. They are here to meet with 30 teenagers for what they call a conversation with a purpose. This area of the city – one of the most deprived – is familiar to some of the visitors (an IT specialist and a young lawyer, a business woman and HR manager, a doctor and an author) because it's where they grew up, and they're back because they want to show the teenagers who are coming after them what happened next in their lives – and what could happen next for them too.

This is Mosaic in action, a small charitable initiative ahead of its time when it was launched by HRH The Prince of Wales in 2007 to raise the aspirations and life chances for young Muslims in the UK. It now boasts nearly 1500 volunteer mentors who go into dozens of schools around the UK. While the charity's demographic is a lot more diverse these days – since the summer of 2016 it became part of the much bigger Prince's Trust – more than 80 per cent of Mosaic's beneficiaries (and they're meeting with about 8000 pupils each year) are still from the 20 per cent of Britain that is most deprived, and many of the British minority ethnic students include young British Muslims. The charity targets those children and young people at risk of floating through school without needing special help (for any learning challenge) or demanding special attention (for their exceptional grades or gifts), and who are often lacking in confidence and at risk of staying right where they are because they and their families don't know what else is out there. Later in the week the students in this school's target group will be whisked off to an international law firm in the city (part of what they call a World of Work visit) so they can discover the kind of jobs on offer there (everything from HR to marketing roles, law to IT) and start to think about the exciting ways they could use what they are learning in class to build a future outside it.

'One of the biggest issues our target groups face is a lack of confidence and aspiration, which we know plays such a big part in attainment,' says Mosaic's Nabila Ayub, who manages and coordinates many of the school visits. 'If their parents are new to the country and English isn't their first language they may not feel able to engage with school or have experience of what university is like and what opportunities are out there. This can inhibit the aspirations and ambitions of their children.'

In primary schools, Mosaic works a lot with mothers and daughters, and says it's often about giving those mothers the chance to see what their daughters could do, to talk about what college or university is like, and what jobs are out there; how they can be combined with being a wife and mother, and with the culture and traditions their families value.

'These workshops are not a parenting class,' says Ayub. 'And they're certainly not about asking parents or students to turn their back on their family or culture. We make that clear. It's about engaging those parents in school life and giving them time, with their daughter, to explore ideas and to build aspirations. We have never had a mother not sign a permission slip for their daughter, but we do see how nervous they are. I remember one mum coming into a session late and upset. She explained later she'd promised her daughter she'd be there but got to the school gate and lost her nerve and turned back. When she got home she mustered up the courage and came rushing back. She never missed another session after that and has gone on to train as a teaching assistant.'

Ayub reckons the students listen to these role models because they know they are valued by them. They also know the mentors have signed up and given their time for free. 'They have no vested interest in the outcomes, but simply don't want the children's and teenagers' future choices to be left to chance when their story could help them fulfil their potential to build a life they love beyond their current experience.'

Back in the Birmingham comprehensive, after the guests have shared their experience, the students are split into groups and assigned an individual role model to work with in sessions planned in advance with the school who can steer themes according to the needs they want to address (be it team building, employability skills, confidence and self-belief).

'Many young people in the UK are lucky and meet role models by chance who inspire and encourage them,' says Ayub. 'But in the majority of cases, especially in these areas where we work, that doesn't happen and young people can end up trapped by their circumstances and never have the kind of conversation they are having in school today. These mentors come back in for several sessions, and slowly help the school open and nourish minds and give students a real sense of their own self-worth. We know that when this happens, and they open their eyes to what they can do next, then we're making a difference.'

What did you call me? Role models on a mission to end bullying

It is, in a sense, a mission to open hearts and minds that brings another set of role models into a secondary school further south, near London. This time, two 30-somethings are standing in front of a class clad with Post-it notes bearing the words the students in the room have confessed they might apply to anyone who is gay or lesbian, bisexual or transgender. The room is silent, the teenagers embarrassed now, seeing the words they so often and easily speak stuck on the famous sportsman and charity CEO – who they now know are both gay – standing in front of them.

These are Diversity Role Models, from the charity of the same name. They are here in this classroom today to talk about homophobia in schools, which they know impacts on students' learning and mental health. Young Minds say more than half of lesbian, gay and bisexual pupils have experienced direct bullying and are left at higher risk of suicide, self-harm and depression. Seven out of ten lesbian and gay students say homophobic bullying impacts on their school work (many skip school because of it) and the Diversity Role Model team know this is often fed by ignorance rather than malice.

Suran Dickson, the teacher who founded and heads up the charity, and who is now standing at the front of the class wearing stickers shouting words like 'faggot', 'queer' and 'loser', was a teacher in a former life. Her class knew she was gay but they liked, trusted and respected her and – as a result – she noticed there was far less gay banter, never mind bullying, in her class. She launched the charity to introduce more children and young people to LGBT adults so they, too, could get to know the person behind the stereotype and so help her reverse the trend of homophobia in Britain's schools. She's since recruited nearly 300 role models and reached over 40,000 pupils in over 150 schools around the UK in workshops like this one.

When the stickers have come off – the stereotypes quickly smashed – the role models walk around the class, talking to pupils about their opinion of people who are gay or seem gay. 'We are simply here to help them think about and discuss their attitudes and how they can feed stereotypes that there is something weird or wrong about being LGBT,' says Dickson. 'They recognise that even gay banter – which they might have thought harmless at the beginning of the session – can make a young person feel they or their family are rubbish or abnormal.' Dickson believes most young people she meets are not homophobic and wouldn't care if their friends were gay or straight, but encourages them to think about how and why they should speak out and stand up for those who are made to feel so bad as a result of the more vocal minority. To think about their own words and the damage they can do. 'You can see the realisation on their faces,' she says. 'Like "yes, that is what I have been saying and that is the hurt I might have caused".'

Dickson also works with teachers, often to develop a diversity policy that is embedded in the curriculum, and to ensure any anti-bullying policy deals directly with homophobic bullying. She says teachers, too, recognise their own fears about even using the word gay, and how they have mistakenly wrapped up sexuality with sex and perhaps become anxious about addressing the issue in class. Despite the fact that nearly all secondary teachers (and two in five primary school teachers) say pupils in their school experience homophobic bullying, nine in ten staff say they've never received any specific training to help them prevent it.

Diversity Role Models is confident about the difference it's making. Not only because of the feedback they get from students in the room (the shift in attitudes is marked and measurable, says Dickson, with 88 per cent saying they would support an LGBT friend and stop using derogatory language) but also via the feedback from the school staff. 'They often say the staff felt the workshops have made the school a nicer place to work, and that they have – in turn – been told by parents they have chosen the school because of this programme. Not because they are gay or have gay children, but because they want to be in a school challenging discrimination and promoting diversity. And we hear, later, about how this has led to other initiatives to promote student wellbeing.

'The work we do is not about sex. It's about relationships and about respect for other people who might be different because they have a different sort of relationship. It's about tackling discrimination, including discrimination based on sexuality, and promoting emotional wellbeing as a result. And that fight is everyone's fight. It's that simple.'

She believes role models can play a powerful role in any PSHE curriculum by providing a human connection that brings an issue to life. 'What happens when you meet someone and like them and learn about their work and get to know them in a workshop? Suddenly who they are, who they love, the colour of their skin, their background, their wealth, their ability or disability doesn't matter any more. None of that matters. And when role models sense that and tell the pupils how life affirming it is to be accepted for who you are, and to have people stand by you and stand up for you, you sense they are empowering everyone who is listening to them to do the same. It is an awesome process to watch.'

Beat is the UK's leading eating disorders charity and in any one year can be in contact with tens of thousands of individuals, supporting anyone (individuals, their friends, families or teachers) affected by eating disorders via their helplines, message boards, resources, workshops and online support groups. To find out about their work, or to arrange a visit from a young ambassador like Chelsea visit www.b-eat.co.uk.

Mosaic delivers three school programmes, two mentoring programmes in primary and secondary schools, and an Enterprise Challenge, a national competition for secondary school students across the UK designed to develop and encourage their entrepreneurial skills. While it doesn't charge for its work in schools, it enlists the support of staff in the school to help deliver the programme. You can find out more about the work it does and how to contact the mentoring teams at www.mosaicnetwork.co.uk.

Diversity Role Models is a national charity working to eliminate homophobic and transphobic bullying and now offers workshops and teacher training to schools around the UK. Their teacher training programme has been designed to specifically support teachers in challenging homophobic bullying and language in schools. They also support head teachers who want to establish an embedded diversity programme across the curriculum and a specific policy tackling homophobic bullying. To find out more visit www.diversityrolemodels.org.

In My View

Rebecca Root and Asad Ahmad on the transformative effects of role models

I am thrilled to be joining DRM as a Patron. If adding my voice helps just one person see the light at the end of the tunnel, or decide to live their life as their authentic self, or find the courage to face the world when everything feels too much – then my voice will have purpose and all my own struggles along the way will have been worth it. When I was young there was nobody to guide or encourage me in the hideous confusion of my gender dysphoria. Thanks to DRM this thankfully is no longer the case.

REBECCA ROOT, ACTOR

The seeds of Mosaic were sown a few years before the official launch in 2007, when I was among several people invited to listen to an idea. HRH The Prince of Wales wanted to find a way of getting young British Muslims, often living in disadvantaged areas, to fulfil their potential by achieving their goals, aims and ambitions. The idea sounded great and so the challenge was set to make it a reality. During a long series of discussions and meetings, I was always impressed with the personal input of the prince through his ideas, comments and questions. Months later, Mosaic was born and I had the honour of hosting the launch. We didn't know what the future would hold, but it is now obvious that there was always a need for British professional Muslims to give others a helping hand in life. After building a firm foundation,

Mosaic is now in a position to continue offering young British Muslims the skills and confidence needed to grow as individuals, enrich the lives of communities and strengthen Britain as a whole.

ASAD AHMAD, BBC NEWS

9

The Mindful Moments

Taking a Breath and Exploring a New Way to Deal with the Pressures of School Life

Making room for mindfulness in your curriculum won't turn off the pressures of life, but it could help children and teenagers take control of how they respond to those pressures. We joined a training session to find out more…

'Children, like adults, feel liberated by knowing that they have the ability to manage better what is going on inside them. By becoming familiar with what is going on in their body and mind, they can help themselves…'
CLAIRE KELLY, MINDFULNESS IN SCHOOLS PROJECT

'So if someone unfriended me on Facebook or didn't like my picture on Instagram then I used to think that it was because they didn't like me, and maybe nobody liked me because I'm such a loser or my photos aren't funny enough. Maybe everyone was talking about me in private chat,' explains Tasha, 13. 'I don't any more.'

'I used to get really stressed in exams or assessments and my mind would close down. I'd start to panic and tell myself I was bound to fail because I couldn't remember anything...because I'm a failure,' says Ryan, 14.

Tasha sniggers at this, and Ryan's friend, Tom, joins in, saying he's learned that most of what his friends say is rubbish and that he shouldn't treat what they tell him as gospel. Ryan and Tash play punch him, laughing.

These children have been commissioned to share what they've learned in their Surrey secondary school this morning, in particular in the mindfulness training they've been having after registration. And while they might joke, there is a sense that this might have been the most important lesson of the day because they're talking about all the things other teenagers say stress them out, but they're talking about them in a very different way.

Children are constantly told to pay attention at school, but they're not usually told how. But today, these teenagers reckon they've tuned into something which is all about paying attention. Not just to specific lessons, such as maths or science, but to the here and now experience of their daily lives. Rather than worry about what's happened before, or could happen next, the lesson today – mindfulness – was all about responding more thoughtfully to what is happening right now.

In another classroom in another school just an hour up the road, a group of teachers are, for a rare moment in the day, still and silent. They are just at the beginning of their own mindfulness training and are learning how to switch off their autopilot. Not just in the corridors and classrooms of this busy academy school in London, but as they wake, walk, eat and drive before they even get here. Paula Kearney, the mindfulness trainer at the front of the class, is part of the Mindfulness in Schools Project (MiSP). Her hope – MiSP's hope – is that the staff will feel the benefits and want to teach the same to their pupils. But even if they don't, the charity knows they'll take the benefits they experience into their life and work and make a difference to those students anyway.

As if in response to this, students at the school approach Paula later saying they can tell which teachers are doing the course, and when asked how, they say they don't really know exactly. They can, they say, just *tell*.

There are many things mental health experts feel should be mandatory in schools, and introduced with a sense of urgency, but mindfulness isn't one of them. Not because it doesn't bring real benefits (more of which below) but because organisations like MiSP know that as soon as schools see it as a tick box exercise it will probably fail, or its shelf life will almost certainly be limited. MiSP doesn't want mindfulness to be seen as another prescribed pressure on teachers' already busy day, but rather to embed this in the culture of the school. To make a lasting impact, MiSP knows it needs time, and it needs teachers who have bought into it and understand the benefits it can bring to the classroom culture in a more organic and lasting way. MiSP offers training in *Paws b*, a scheme for 7–11-year-olds and *.b* ('dot-bee') for secondary school children, and the ideal, they say, would be to see teachers then use 'mindfulness moments' throughout the day in assemblies, the playground, class and staff rooms – and teach and encourage children to do the same.

Which brings us back to the teachers sitting in this room trying to discover how to press pause.

'Schools are stressful places to work, and becoming more stressful all the time as a result of additional testing, assessments, inspections and policy changes,' says Paula Kearney. 'What's more, teachers are dealing with humans all day long and so can never predict what might happen next. That causes them to live in a reactive state which can feed stress and create a cycle of behaviour where everything becomes an issue.'

Mindfulness, on the other hand, encourages us to pause rather than react, and to assess quietly what is happening and the best way to respond to it. 'I think that's what students probably pick up on when they second-guess which staff have been on the course,' says Kearney. 'Young people are often more intuitive than adults and when they see teachers being less reactive, and able to respond more calmly to different things that are thrown at them, they *feel* the difference.'

While mindfulness originated in Buddhist thinking and meditation practice thousands of years ago, the mindfulness we're seeing now – and certainly the mindfulness brought into classrooms via programmes like *.b* – is secular and simple, and based on well-researched and evidence-based mindfulness programmes including mindfulness-based cognitive therapy. Over its 10-week course, MiSP delivers a set of distinct skills teachers can learn on their lunch break or children can practise while sitting at their desks or in assembly. Students (old or young) gradually learn to direct their attention in a more focused way to what is happening – in their breathing, sensations, thoughts and feelings, what they're eating, how they're moving around – and to do it with what MiSP term open-minded curiosity and acceptance. It's not about turning off any pressure they're under (and of course in schools some pressure and adrenalin is healthy), but about teaching them not to be driven by it, not to be overwhelmed by what just happened or what might happen next. It is designed to give the mindful a choice in how they respond to what's happening, good and bad. With practice, it makes those choices ever more thoughtful and skilful, says MiSP. The effects can include an enhanced sense of calm and improved focus and concentration.

Mindfulness has been in the headlines a lot of late, as it has found its way into mainstream medicine, psychology, social care and healthcare. Celebrities such as Ruby Wax have talked about how they've used it to combat depression, businesses are investing heavily in the idea to promote staff wellbeing and more patients than ever are now being referred to it. It's now recommended by the National Institute of Clinic Excellence, for example, to deal with issues such as stress, anxiety and depression. In 2015 evidence from an all-party Parliamentary group was conveyed in the report Mindful Nation UK, looking at its role in health policy, and now a Wellcome Foundation funded study is setting out to measure the impact it can have.

Here in school, MiSP says different children get different things out of mindfulness but is clear that this should never be considered a panacea for mental health issues, or even an intervention in the traditional sense as counselling might be. 'Our curricula are delivered to the whole class or year group as a way of acknowledging that everyone gets anxious sometimes, and everyone struggles with that,' says Claire Kelly, the charity's director of content and training. 'It is not about simply stopping difficult thoughts or behaviour, but showing young people how to work differently with those thoughts so they can grow and flourish.' So, for example, she suggests it helps students notice when their mind wanders, notice when they're on autopilot, and notice a strong reaction to someone or something. Having learned to notice, it shows them how to draw on skills and develop those skills to give them back some control. 'That is when you see this wonderful stepping back in children,' she says. 'They're noticing their thinking rather than getting caught up in it.'

While not considered an intervention for any 'target' group, Kelly does recall teaching a group of boys who struggled with attention and were disrupting the session. They pulled everyone's focus away to such a degree they were given the chance to leave the group and go and do something else. She then delivered some small group training to them afterwards. 'I wanted them to recognise the mature choice they'd made in leaving the group rather than disrupting it, but also help them feel valued and part of what we were trying to do,' she says. The next time the boys were in a session they were, she says, a lot more focused. 'What was a real revelation was how one of the boys responded during this session on the amygdala (our fight or flight response) and strategies to use when it might cause people to kick off. He started getting anxious, clenching his fists and rocking slightly. He stood up, looked at his feet, and said "That was my amygdala, wasn't it? My prefrontal cortex is working now." The teacher and I just looked at each other. Having spent his life being removed from classrooms he couldn't cope with, he seemed to be discovering a tool within him to manage the situation better, simply because he now understood what was happening to him.

'Children, like adults, feel liberated by knowing that they have the ability to manage better what is going on inside them. By becoming familiar with what is going on in their body and mind, they can help themselves,' she says.

That's not to undermine kids who are having a really difficult time, explains Kelly. 'We know those children are part of every school and will often need more targeted interventions and expert support,' she says. 'But mindfulness doesn't discourage that; it adds to it. We see it as a powerful part of the package of measures schools can adopt to promote good mental health.'

In fact, MiSP believes one of the most wonderful aspects about teaching mindfulness curricula to the whole class is that it makes every child feel part of a community, and helps them recognise that they are not alone in their struggles. 'The inclusivity of mindfulness isn't explicit, but there is a recognition when you see children practising it that they all share common concerns and anxieties. And that is a lovely way of bringing people together,' says Kelly. 'There is a shared language (for example when they talk about FOFBOC – feet on floor bottom on chair), and a shared interest in sharing what has been learned with others.'

She also believes mindfulness in schools can help counter issues we know can aggravate mental health problems, such as the pressure that comes from social media. 'We never demonise it – in fact we utilise social media to reach children via apps and YouTube links – but want to help children notice the pull and their reaction to what they read or listen to. Children can feel they are being dragged along by others' ideas, frustrated about being in one place in their life when they think they should be in another.

'We want them to understand it doesn't have to be that way, and to be more mindful about how they respond to those pressures around them,' she says. 'We want mindfulness to help them recognise they don't have to compare themselves to others or believe what those others are saying about them. That there are other ways, better ways, to see the situation they're in.'

Kelly knows some schools might be sceptical about the benefits, and the time they'd need to invest. In response, MiSP has a wealth of studies it can direct schools to, including those of Professor Katherine Weare who has researched the impact of mindfulness in over 500 teenagers and found that those who completed the programme saw improvements in terms of stress, anxiety and wellbeing, even three months after the intervention.

'Again, we know mindfulness won't make the difference it could or should unless teachers have felt the benefits, which is why we'd recommend any school starts by getting a course – even a taster session on an INSET day – for their staff,' says Kearney, who has already seen their organisation take training to thousands of teachers in the UK. 'Once they practise and experience the benefits outside this class they almost always want to go on from their own training and do more, for themselves and for the pupils they teach.'

To find out more about **mindfulness**, and how it could support children and teenagers in your school, visit https://mindfulnessinschools.org. *Paws b* is a scheme for 7–11-year-olds and *.b* for secondary school children. Via the website your school can find a trained teacher, arrange a taster day, organise staff training and learn how to teach mindfulness to pupils.

A Mindfulness Guide for the Frazzled by Ruby Wax, published by Penguin, is a brilliant guide to this new way of thinking and includes a section for children and teenagers drawing on some of the author's favourite exercises from the *.b* curricula developed by the Mindfulness in Schools Project. Visit www.penguin.co.uk for more information.

In My View

Kate Griggs on a campaign to help children with dyslexia thrive

Kate Griggs is founder and CEO of Made by Dyslexia, a new charity championing change in the way we understand and support children with dyslexia.

We are all aware that there is a link between children's learning challenges like dyslexia and their mental health (we see a high instance, for example, of anxiety in these pupils) and we are now starting to understand what goes wrong, early on. Feeling that you're failing has a huge impact on children – and children with dyslexia can start to feel like failures as soon as they start school. Almost all the dyslexic young people and adults I speak to (and I count myself in this group) felt out of sync the minute they got into school, and started to feel like a failure not long after.

Teachers learn in college how these early years are critical for the development of self-confidence as children are given opportunities for approval and recognition from their peers and from the key adults in their life. They know how, when self-confidence starts to build, children persevere and take pleasure in their work as they move through the school. They also know that children who feel they're not meeting expectations, or know they're not keeping up with their peers, can feel inferior – and that sense of self-worth, which should be growing as they move through school, can be badly damaged at a critical time.

Yet teachers are, reluctantly, having to test children more (phonics check aged five/six, Key Stage 1, SATs at six/seven and Key Stage 2 SATS and Spag – spelling, punctuation and grammar and times tables – at 10/11) and are under huge pressure to shape learning so children can get through those tests. This not only causes a huge amount of stress, but also distracts, if not destroys altogether, opportunities to embed things like creativity via art and music. It can also prevent teachers handing on practical learning which could go hand in hand with reading and writing. This all has a cumulative, negative impact on all children; but particularly those with challenges like dyslexia who are characteristically creative, empathetic, imaginative, practical and full of ideas they'd like to explore. They can be left behind and made to feel stupid because those tests are all about rote learning and things they struggle with – and ignore all the things they excel in which should be encouraged and developed.

We wouldn't inflict something like this on children at this age if it had an impact on their physical health, but the system seems set on forcing children to do things which are clearly having an effect on their mental health. It is no surprise that so many children with dyslexia have anxiety disorders and are labelled as having behavioural problems; and no surprise that the focus then shifts onto social difficulties or family issues that might be underneath them, rather than what is going on in class.

Made by Dyslexia wants to change that. We want dyslexia to be properly understood as a range of difficulties *and* skills. We want to see all dyslexic pupils identified early and properly supported so we can harness their talents and build their self-esteem. Teachers we speak to want that too. They know that if they can recognise and nurture children's individual talents, they can achieve their greatest results.

Made by Dyslexia is a global movement led by successful dyslexics, bringing together charities, thought leaders and educators united behind three global goals for dyslexia:

- that dyslexia is properly understood as a range of difficulties *and* skills

- that *all* teachers are trained to support dyslexic pupils

- that *all* dyslexic pupils are identified and properly supported.

The charity is building an online platform with tools that will support and enable their three global goals and are campaigning for changes in testing and exams.

www.madebydyslexia.org

10

The Community Project
Helping Pupils Realise Just How Much They're Worth

Children and teenagers are full of energy and talent and yet not enough of them get to use it to do great things for other people. Step Up To Serve's #iwill campaign wants to change that, and give every young person a real sense of their worth. Three schools explain what they learned when they signed up.

'The pressure on young people [in this area] is immense, self esteem chronically low and mental health issues massively on the rise...there are all sorts of explanations for why that's happened, but we know we have to deal with the situation we're in and help pupils deal with the pressure they're under. Our job is to build them up.'
                    MIKE WHITTINGHAM, HAYWOOD ACADEMY

Ameena Khan is at the far end of the hospital ward, smoothing sheets while she makes up a bed with a colleague. As she walks back to the nursing station two patients call out and she turns to talk quietly to one lady, smiling as she fills her water glass, before attending to another woman who is hard of hearing, lifting her tiny voice to explain when the doctor is next doing a round. For this 16-year-old, today is another Thursday at college, but not as most teenagers know it. For three days every week Ameena is part of a team on this elder care ward at this huge hospital in Stoke-on-Trent, arriving by bus at the start of her six-hour shift, wearing – like her new colleagues – a uniform of flat shoes, pale blue scrub trousers and nurse's tunic.

'On my first day I was so nervous. I brought in my lunch but wasn't sure if I was allowed to eat with the nurses or what I would be able to do to help here,' says Ameena. 'But that changed so quickly. When you are doing a job like this with people – learning to clean, change beds, care for patients – you become part of the team. You *feel* part of the team and work together to get the job done.'

'By the end of the second week we saw a huge transformation,' says a nurse passing by with a trolley. 'Ameena was so shy. But she is a real asset to us. And the patients love her. They are always asking for the "nurse with the headscarf" (Ameena wears a black hijab).'

'I knew this was going to be different from school pretty quickly,' says Ameena. 'I have learned a lot of new things about myself, including what I can offer and how much fun learning new skills can be. I feel so much more confident inside. I want a job like this when I leave college.'

Down the road Ameena's classmate Megan is supporting a class of 28 primary school children, helping the teacher in charge run a reading session in the library, while across the city their classmate Jamie is working at an IT firm. In fact, this once industrial heartland, famous for centuries of pottery making, now has dozens of young people like them whose schooling involves three days a week in the workplace. The other two they're back at college packing in a timetable of employability skills, English, maths, budgeting, food and more, all designed to prepare them for the independent working life that's waiting round the corner.

This kind of voluntary workplace learning isn't a new thing but, here at Haywood Academy, one of Stoke-on-Trent's largest secondary schools, the staff are running the biggest programme of its type in the country and on a mission to give pupils not wanting or able to take the traditional academic route through A Levels the opportunity to do something for others and to make something of themselves. Some 50 plus – more than a third of the school's sixth form cohort – are currently on the programme.

Haywood Academy is also one of scores of schools which have signed up to the #iwill campaign, coordinated by the charity Step Up To Serve. Launched in 2013 and championed by HRH The Prince of Wales, it not only aims to promote the benefits of social action but, via collaboration with businesses, the education and voluntary sectors, embed it in all 10–20-year-olds' life journeys. The cross-sector campaign is on a mission to see at least 60 per cent of young people both adding something to their own community, and realising their own value to it, by the year 2020.

'We sensed at the beginning there was little understanding in schools of the real benefits and variety of social action outside the Duke of Edinburgh's Award,' says the charity's education manager, Kerri Hall. 'Only about four in ten youngsters are currently involved in social action and we wanted to change that. Most of those involved got into it through school, so we know that is the best place for us to start.'

Developing critical skills and character qualities

The charity knew this could never be a simple tick box exercise, with pupils going off to volunteer for an odd afternoon sorting coats in a charity shop or raising money through an annual school fair. They knew they had to engage with leaders, who would recognise that every young person (not just those familiar or comfortable with the concept of volunteering) has something positive to contribute. The pre-launch consultation developed key principles that underpin the quality of the social action experience and included the need for any project to have a real social impact, be youth-led, and be in tune with a young person's passions and ambitions. It had to be challenging, progressive and embedded into a young person's life, with opportunity for them to reflect on the benefits to them and the impact to others.

All the evidence they've collected since[1] suggests something wonderful happens when social action works to this formula. Emerging evidence shows that young people who take part develop some of the most critical skills and character qualities needed for life and transition into adulthood. The research demonstrates an increase in resilience and prosocial behaviour with issues such as anxiety reduced and wellbeing and empathy enhanced.

Employers who back the #iwill campaign know that a lack of any job or the skills to get one are among the biggest pressures on young people today, and supporting them to change that a key way of promoting mental health. Step Up To Serve's studies show that eight out of ten youngsters taking part in social action say they're capable of more than they realised, and three quarters feel more confident about getting a job as a result. Meanwhile, more than two thirds of employers say candidates with social action experience demonstrate better employability skills.

'Social action is not about telling young people what to do, but rather trusting them and giving them responsibility and the chance to see what they have to contribute,' says Kerri Hall. 'That

---

1   Ipsos Mori Youth Social Action in the UK (2015) for the Cabinet Office and Step Up To Serve Behavioural Insight's Team: Evaluating Youth Social Action.

doesn't mean the projects have to be huge, like the kind we're seeing at Haywood. It can happen in school in small ways. We've seen the power of everything from playground buddies to promote inclusion, to a political campaign run by year 5s who wanted to clean up a bridge near their school to make it a safer place to cross. But when it's done well it helps young people feel connected. The benefits can be empowering and transformative and stay with them for life.'

Haywood Academy's head teacher, Carl Ward, and his deputy head, Mike Whittingham (who helped create and now leads the programme), decided to bring social action and their commitment to #iwill into their workplace training model and are seeing how powerful their sixth form could be. Stoke-on-Trent is listed as one of the most 20 deprived areas in England and has suffered decades of economic stagnation, a shortfall in skills and educational attainment.

'We are seeing third and fourth generation unemployed; youngsters from families who could be relying on food banks to eat, and young people coming here with extremes of needs. The pressure on them is immense, self-esteem chronically low and mental health issues massively on the rise,' says Mike Whittingham. 'There are all sorts of explanations for why that's happened but we know we have to deal with the situation we're in and help pupils deal with the pressure they're under, from their peers and families and the outside world. They know the expectation is to get five GCSEs and go to college. So if they don't succeed they can feel their standing in the community and within their family is gone. That knocks their confidence in a dangerous way. Our job is to build them up, to give them a step up.'

Whittingham worked long and hard presenting his ideas to local businesses and organisations (from the NHS to the financial sector, education to retail) knowing his students had to be part of, and not superfluous (and sitting around waiting for things to do), if the work was to build their skills and confidence. He was overwhelmed by how much they embraced and wanted to be part of the programme. 'Not only so they could find skilled employees to train up, but so they could support the social action element of what we were trying to do and get behind something that could help regenerate the city,' he says. Now his pupils are interviewed to secure each individual post, required to turn up at set times, adhere to dress or uniform code, have a specific role and are learning a prescribed set of skills. Crucially, he says, unlike the odd week or month's work experience, or even a three-month traineeship, his students can be in post for anywhere up to a year with a view to being snapped up for apprenticeships in the city. This is something that's already bearing fruit for the first cohort of volunteers.

'We want to support pupils, including the most disadvantaged students with quality life skills,' says Whittingham. 'They need to leave here understanding their wages, tax, how to catch the bus, how to keep themselves healthy. We want to give them choices through knowledge and experience, rather than see them held back by a lack of it.'

But he also recognises that the first thing most of the youngsters learn (and what nearly all of them most value) is the confidence in themselves, and the sense they are making a difference to the team they're a part of, the workplace they're in, and the community where they are based. 'That in itself is transformational,' he says. 'Aspiration is massive and self-belief is essential. Some students take to it like ducks to water, but there are others who don't feel they are worth anything and have chronically low confidence, so it can be more of a challenge to get them settled. But we are determined not to give in. We have a pastoral care team and will support students through interview, drive them to work to get them settled, visit them at home if they don't turn up, and at work to check they're okay and to monitor progress. We don't want any student to fail.

'Ameena is a classic example of someone who needed support to take the route she's taken. She's grabbed this opportunity at the hospital with both hands and is flourishing. The impact on her confidence is amazing, and she's using that confidence to learn more effectively when she's back in the classroom.'

At another hospital, a little further up the M6, pupils from a local primary school are busy serving food on the children's ward. This is a termly event using a healthy menu the pupils design, develop and then cook in the hospital kitchens, serving up trays of food to children their own age. It's part of a parcel of social action now operating at Victoria Academy in Barrow-in-Furness, Cumbria. The children explain how they've just raised money to make ready-made hampers for families who rely on food banks, delivered with their own personal letters and triggering plenty back.

'The children were just amazed by the letters they received, and by the impact they'd had,' says their head teacher, Caroline Vernon. 'And so one project inspires the next.'

Victoria Academy is one of a long and growing list of primary schools which is championing the #iwill campaign's vision to inspire social action at a younger age. Like Haywood's sixth form, the driver at Vernon's school was to raise children's aspirations at a time when the recession was rearing its head in the classroom, with pupils talking about how hard things were at home, and how rubbish they considered Barrow as a place to live. Like Haywood, they turned to the business community to get them started.

'The school launched a project with local business men and women who came in and worked in the classroom, challenging the children to find out what they did and the part it played in making Barrow-in-Furness a good place to be,' says Caroline Vernon. 'What it taught us was the power of making learning real and relevant to children's lives, and the power of building connections with the community.'

Education for citizenship

So at this school in Cumbria a skills-based curriculum underpins the academic one, and the children are taught in a business-like model, working on their studies collaboratively as a team.

'We see what we call Business and Enterprise Education as a way to foster and develop core skills through real situations and to promote education for citizenship,' she says. 'That not only includes partnerships with businesses but with parents so children can benefit from their knowledge and skills.'

Her staff organise children into working teams making sure everyone recognises each others' roles, and that it's okay not to be good at everything. They've all been taught that to work as a team they have to identify each others' strengths so everyone can be the best they can be for the good of that team, and so everyone can develop new skills throughout the exercise. They've also learnt to recognise when they need help. 'They'll think about where they can look for that help and know they can call on "experts" from the community (they might nominate each others' parents or grandparents) who can add to their learning and help them with the project or campaign they are working on.'

The impact on learning and behaviour was soon clear, says Vernon (there was a huge rise in attendance and less incidence of disruptive behaviour, for instance). This led the school into more proactive social action (including projects such as hospital food and hampers). 'The work we were doing with business aligned to the skills needed to build character and to deliver youth social action,' she says. 'A genuine sense of pride for and ownership of the school community came out of this, and the children built on that by caring for each other – and for the teachers.

'I notice when new children arrive the pupils work to help them become part of the school. They talk about the way we work with real pride. And when children are mean, as all children can be sometimes, the majority view is that it's not on, that you don't have to be mean to be top dog. There is no top dog. That isn't how this school operates.'

At Newton Farm Nursery, Infant and Junior School in Harrowhead, teacher Rekha Bhakoo recognises that shift in culture. She runs a rights respecting school and sees social action as part of the daily timetable.

'The children decide what they want to improve in the community and galvanise our support to do it,' she says. 'When they thought they might lose the library they wrote to their MP and were part of a campaign that led to the library now being run via a volunteer programme.'

The school recently ran a fundraising project, too, where every child was given five pounds and had to use it to make something to sell at a profit. It was something that infiltrated numeracy, literacy, design and technology. They made everything from pencil cases to gift cards and then worked out how much they'd spent, how much they'd made, the profit and where they should put it.

'We are supporting a special school in Kenya; we've helped build it brick by brick, so no surprise they all wanted the money to go there,' says Bhakoo. 'Through this school project they've learned the value of water and the way a community can use farming to become self-sufficient. We get photos and letters from the children who go there. But by doing this via the curriculum everyone is engaged and everyone benefits. There is a real sense of joy when they see what they have done for others.'

'The schools that have signed up – and there are scores like them – are making social action part of the fabric of the school,' says Step Up To Serve's Kerri Hall. 'That ensures the benefits reach every young person, not just those who would sign up for a project anyway, or the families who are always helping out at fundraisers. When it works well social action becomes part of what it means to be a pupil or student at that school.'

'I can see how this has given the children a sense of their own worth and built their self-belief,' says Caroline Vernon. 'At Victoria Academy we try and build on this by making their dreams and ambitions real. We've been working with the local college so the children can go in for the day, buddy up with a student and get a taste of what it's like to train. They can pick something they're interested in, be it hairdressing or engineering or art. They do their own CV and apply for a placement in line with their skills. We raised money so they could wear the work gear – the overalls or beauticians' tunics – their buddies did on the courses.

'We also ran a project with BAE Systems, who design and build submarines for the Royal Navy at their site in Barrow,' explains Caroline. Her pupils had to design something that floated, sank and then came back up, and work out how to market it. They were put into teams and assigned jobs – a designer, quality checker, media person, etc. – each team had to present their idea to staff at BAE. The winning team got to present to the BAE directors in the boardroom.

'It was amazing to see the children sitting in front of the directors of this international company, their little legs dangling from these huge chairs as they confidently explained the academic principles of their project. I don't think those kids will remember their SATs results, but they will remember that feeling of being heard, of being part of something that was valued, of having a taste of how they could contribute to something big in their own community.'

#iwill is a national campaign led by organisations across every sector who have pledged to support more young people to get involved in social action. The campaign has found out from education leaders up and down the country what schools can do to develop and embed social action. Its research partners can demonstrate some of the key benefits – including improved wellbeing and confidence – that social action can deliver.

Step Up To Serve, the charity which coordinates the campaign, knows that many young people are already doing fantastic things in their community, but wants to see others playing their part so all young people have access to opportunities and can enjoy the benefits, including new skills, more confidence, enhanced self-worth and improved employability skills.

Many schools are now working with local charities, businesses and wider organisations but others are using their own school-based campaigns or fundraising initiatives to deliver the benefits of social action to their pupils. To hear from other school leaders who've signed up, and to read about what they've done, visit http://education.iwill.org.uk. If you'd like to find out more, visit their website at www.iwill.org.uk, which has a series of resources to support your school.

11

The Run

The 15-Minute Exercise that's Promoting Mental Health

All the evidence shows the positive impact of exercise on our mental as well as physical health. Yet children are more inactive than ever. Could a daily run around the playground be the cheapest, simplest way to promote wellbeing?

'The beauty of this, and the real benefit, is in its simplicity. Everyone finds it easy to manage and everyone, including the teachers, feels better. And when everyone feels better, why would they want to stop?'
DUNCAN SETTERINGTON, ACTIVE CHESHIRE

As you walk through the gate of Horn's Mill Primary School in Cheshire you are greeted by a trail of red, black and white – scores of children snaking around the playground. Some are running and chatting hand in hand, others walking beside their teacher engrossed in a debate, and there are gaggles of pupils, faces bursting with effort and excitement, looking like they're training for a marathon.

This is Horn's Mill's version of the Daily Mile, the concept that hit the headlines when a school in Stirling revealed that the introduction of a daily run (quite separate from PE, break or lunchtime play) had improved the health of every child in the school. Crucially though, the pupils at the school were not only fitter, said the reports, but they were happier too. Attention levels and behaviour in class had improved.

It sounds so easy and so sensible that some might wonder how it made it into the national press and TV headlines. Don't most school children run about every day?

But this – the Daily Mile – was different, and what made it worthy of its headline was the fact that it had been sustained week after week for three years.

One organisation looking on was Active Cheshire which works with schools in Cheshire and Warrington on interventions to help children get more active.

'We were intrigued,' says Duncan Setterington, Active Cheshire's strategic lead for education. 'We know schools get ideas thrown at them left right and centre. They might pick them up and give them a go for a while, but then they disappear, kicked into touch by things considered higher priority on the curriculum. The 'nice to have and nice to do projects' can be the first to go when pressure mounts. But this was three years in...'

So Active Cheshire ventured up to St Ninian's, the school in Stirling which created the Daily Mile, to discover its secret; determined to bring back the benefits to thousands of children in their area.

What they found was something as straightforward as the name on the tin, but with something special at its heart. St Ninian's told Active Cheshire they had, quite simply, placed health and wellbeing at the 'top of their pyramid of priorities'.

Before they started the Daily Mile, it seems three things – literacy, numeracy and safe and happy pupils – were the core elements of their school plan. Then they added health and wellbeing – both physical and mental – into the mix. When they did, they saw how it impacted on the happiness of their pupils, and on their achievements in the classroom.

'So health and wellbeing climbed right to the top of the pyramid, above everything else,' says Setterington. 'That's the ethos of the school and so the Daily Mile is absolutely integral to every day. The children are healthier, fitter, happier and more focused.'

He also saw how, three years on, the Daily Mile had grown organically into something that fitted seamlessly into the day. St Ninian's explained that key to its success was each teacher having ownership of the run, and the flexibility to use it as they saw fit. 'It's a learning tool they can use to suit the flow of the class, the rhythm of the day, and even the mood of the moment. If the class isn't engaged or is disruptive or lethargic each teacher can, without consultation, down tools and lead their pupils outside for their run.'

Rules of the run

There were some fundamental practicalities too. Good weather is seen as a bonus, but bad weather isn't a barrier to the run, explains Setterington. The pupils don't need to change into their PE kit, or even change their shoes. There's no queuing up at various entrances and exits along the way or crowd control in the corridors that might disrupt other classes. At St Ninian's the children form one queue at their class door and then simply feed into the playground and straight onto their circuit round the field. When the 15 minutes is up the teacher heads back to class and the children follow. This not only saves time, and keeps the process running smoothly, it also prevents any sense of competition.

'This isn't the place for children to compete,' says Setterington. 'There's no starting line, no first or last. Look at the children here. They can choose to run or walk, on their own or as a group. Every child succeeds every day. And because they move in this natural flow as they come out to the Mile they are often chatting to pupils outside their playground friendship group which is good for promoting friendships and inclusion, too. Some like to walk with the teacher one day but the next race round in a sprint.'

'One of the emotional benefits is the space it creates for pupils to mix with each other and to talk to their teachers in a new way,' says Horn's Mill's head teacher, Sharon Wyatt, as she watches children run round the playground in Helsby. 'In the busy life that is the primary classroom some children struggle to come up to the teacher and chat about what's on their mind. But on the Daily Mile we see them do that every day, and teachers who sense a child needs some TLC will take the opportunity to chat to them too.'

Horn's Mill is one of six pilot schools in West Cheshire and is already demonstrating its confidence in the Mile's future by planning to move the route from ten laps around the playground to a new all-weather circuit around the edge of the school field. But Setterington wants to see every school in West Cheshire – over 90 – following suit by the end of July 2017. The head teachers from the six pilots are, with Active Cheshire and both the local council's public health team and NHS Clinical Commissioning Group, presenting the concept (and the benefits they've felt) to colleagues across the county.

'Our six pilot schools are being monitored by the public health team. They're measuring physical impact, children's enjoyment of the run, and their teacher's view of its impact on their wellbeing and focus in class. We want to present this to other schools so they can get going as quickly as possible. And yes, we anticipate they'll start as we did with the question "Is this it? Can it be that simple?" And we anticipate they might want to complicate it by talking about competitions and certificates they could hand out in assembly. But that misses the point. The beauty of this, and the real benefit, is in its simplicity. Everyone finds it easy to manage and everyone, including the teachers, feels better. And when everyone feels better, why would they want to stop?

'Children's lives are more sedentary nowadays,' says Horn's Mill's Sharon Wyatt. 'Many primary head teachers I know struggle with traffic outside school because the vast majority of pupils come to school in the car. We sometimes hear children complaining about being tired or having aching legs on a short two-mile walk through town. People rightly talk about the impact this has on issues like childhood obesity, but it's easy to overlook the impact on children's emotional health.'

Exercise has long linked the body and mind, working to keep both healthy. It is one of the key things promoted by charities such as Young Minds. Scientists know that a daily dose of exercise triggers the release of feel-good chemicals in the brain. And research has shown that physical activity can be as good as antidepressants or psychological treatments like cognitive behavioural therapy (CBT).

'But we know it's not as simple as saying, go join a gym or sign up to a football team,' says Setterington. 'If people associate it with sport, and they hate sport and its associations with success or failure, they won't be interested. It has to be about connecting with people in the right way, putting their needs and their way of exercising first. It's the same with school pupils. There are bound to be youngsters who don't enjoy PE, or aren't the ones their peers pick for the team. Exercise for mental wellbeing has to find a way into their lives in a regular way, and in a format they can enjoy. I really believe St Ninian's sustain their programme – and we're sustaining ours – because we leave it up to the children to choose how they complete the mile, and for these 15 minutes there is no pressure on them at all. We don't want or need to over-test it. If they keep exercising like this, day after day, week after week, term after term that is an end in itself. They will feel the benefits and come to see it as a habit for life. They will be healthier – that has to happen. That is some result.'

Elaine Wyllie, the head teacher who launched the **Daily Mile** in Stirling, is now retired and promotes the idea to others in education via her own charity. It offers resources for any schools wanting to give it a try. For more information visit www.thedailymile.co.uk.

In My View

Suzy Greaves on the campaign to make PSHE statutory

Suzy Greaves is editor of Psychologies, *the women's magazine which is seeing readership rise year on year. Their success comes at a time when the nation's interest in positive mental health and everything that contributes to it comes into focus.* Psychologies *is also one of many magazine titles that have signed up to the campaign to make PSHE statutory in schools.*

We know our readers not only want to understand their relationship with the world around them, but how to flourish in it. That is the same for children and young people, which is why, for me, PSHE is the most important subject on the timetable.

Children and young people not only need to learn the facts (about how their body and brain works and how to care for them, about what makes a healthy relationship, about the world of work, about other cultures, other families, other generations) but to learn the skills that will help them listen, question and connect with others in a positive way. They need to understand how and why they should embrace diversity, the power of kindness and ways to celebrate difference. Confidence comes with this kind of competence. It is what will empower them to engage in honest discussion about the world and drive change. It is how they will learn to connect to their own inner compass, so they can make choices that are right for them. When they hit tough times – and everyone hits tough times – they can understand what depression or stress or anxiety look and feel like and what to do about them. They'll know what help is out there, and how to ask for it. Surely these are the most important things we can teach children and young people today.

We have come a long way. There was a time when there was shame and stigma associated with mental health issues. But look at the organisations out there promoting it, the articles being written about it, the people talking about their own mental health in the public arena. Look at the way the three young royals – three dynamic young mentors – have launched the campaign Heads Together, so we can open up this issue and recognise how everyone struggles.

We still have a long way to go, though. If you want to think about the economics, the numbers stack up. The cost of not prioritising children and young people's emotional wellbeing is clear. The power of an enlightened education system could not only save the country millions, it could change everything for the better.

12

The PSHE Lesson

Rethinking the Subject that Will Help You Shape What Happens Next

If mental health matters, why isn't the subject that tackles this issue most directly a statutory one? In this final chapter, the PSHE Association and a school that's supporting its case for change explain the role this subject can play in promoting emotional wellbeing.

'[Pupils find] their voice, an inner confidence in themselves, and an ability to listen to others and ask for help from adults when they need it. It's not an overnight thing, but it seeps into their learning (about themselves and others) in these sessions, and translates into an ability to work better across the curriculum.'
DI HARRILL, NEWENT SECONDARY SCHOOL

On the wall of a school in Newent, Gloucestershire, a poster shouts out *It might not be easy, but it will be worth it!*, which seems appropriate given that this is the PSHE classroom, and that this is the subject that tends to get batted about by staff (the short straw gets to teach it), and can get pushed off the timetable when extra maths or science or something else considered more pressing takes precedence. So much so that this whole classroom – designated a PSHE wing – is pretty unusual as secondary schools go.

The poster is meant for the pupils, of course, designed to move and motivate, rather than to support those battling to get PSHE on the timetable as a statutory subject. The message is surrounded by others from the '*Some people are trans – get over it*' to '*How an act of kindness can change the world*'. There are posters about bullying, budgeting, healthy consent in sex, dementia and drugs. And next door, the PSHE office has shelves lined with resources – scores of DVDs with documentaries and films covering an equally diverse range of subjects. There's also a wall lined with the PSHE timetables, alongside a schedule of visiting speakers. It seems in this particular secondary school in Newent, Gloucestershire, the battle is being won.

Many teachers across the country are alarmed by the way their timetable appears to be skewed towards a knowledge-based curriculum and almost all believe that PSHE education – Personal, Social, Health and Economic education – has a crucial part to play in creating a more holistic approach to school life. Yet PSHE is still not statutory and – as a result – not a single teacher in the UK trains to be a PSHE teacher at college (even though tens of thousands deliver the lessons) – schools are simply left to decide who picks up sessions (sometimes teaching assistants if teachers are too busy), and what's on the curriculum. Ofsted's most recent report suggested subjects such as mental health and online safety might be left out altogether and, as a result, millions of children miss out on high quality lessons or are left at risk as a result of poorly taught ones. This situation surely needs to change.

Left to contemplate the government's stance, some teachers have taken matters into their own hands. Di Harrill, Newent Community School's head of PSHE, and many like her in the

UK, have tenaciously campaigned for a PSHE department with a promise from her leadership team that every pupil gets at least one 50-minute session a week, together with an assurance that if something has to give in the timetable it's not automatically her lesson. They're now things she vehemently defends because it's here in this poster-clad classroom she knows her pupils can develop a different type of knowledge and understanding, and learn a different set of skills – skills kids need to manage their lives, now and in the future.

Delivering skills for life

'The lesson itself gives them space to think about and discuss specific issues, but it's the core skills they develop – assertiveness and communication, problem solving and negotiation skills – that help them thrive,' says Harrill. 'That's what other teachers notice first – the fact that pupils have found their voice, an inner confidence in themselves, and an ability to listen to others and ask for help from adults when they need it. It's not an overnight thing, but it seeps into their learning (about themselves and others) in these sessions, and translates into an ability to work better across the curriculum. It can have an impact on the whole ethos of the school.'

There are bigger things going on in this county too. Harrill is in a team of teachers leading Gloucestershire's Healthy Living and Learning Initiative. Launched in 2012, it's seen by many as a response to the continuing lack of statutory PSHE provision, and the government's move away from the Every Child Matters agenda. It now brings free training, resources and support to schools across the county via the county's own 'PSHE and safeguarding curriculum' called PINK (People in the Know).

PINK aims to capture and deliver all areas of PSHE education, which is, of course, designed to put a spotlight on and help children learn about real-life issues which affect them, their families and communities, and to help them manage many of the most critical opportunities, challenges and responsibilities they'll face growing up. As illustrated in the Newent PSHE wing, that can cover everything from debt to domestic abuse, drugs to dementia, consensual sex to being a young carer, writing a CV to starting work. It delivers ideas that challenge myths and misconceptions pupils might have picked up on TV soaps, in the playground, on the school bus, or via the internet. It's lessons taught here that promote children's mental health most directly, not only via classes, which discuss topics directly, but by signposting information and support, and by reducing mental health stigma by opening up the subject in an honest and direct way.

'I thought debt was something only affecting poor people or those out of work,' says Callum, 15, 'but I've recognised that someone who drives a fancy BMW and wears the best clothes can have their life ruined by debt, by not managing their money and taking advice.'

Kim, who has just turned 16, says, 'I honestly didn't realise that most girls my age don't want to have sex, and I was secretly worried that it was kind of a requirement of the third date.' She adds, 'You see all this stuff about what boys want and what girls are supposed to look like, and even if you read other articles trying to give you confidence to be yourself it's kind of a relief to know what other girls and boys are thinking, and what they want out of relationships.'

Simon and Erin, both 15 and in year 10, have been talking about learning disabilities and how they've come to understand issues such as autism, and how they might react better when they see other young people struggling in the street or the supermarket or in the workplace. Meanwhile, Dave wants to work in theatre and says he looked online at the amazing things theatres are doing to make them autism- or dementia-friendly.

So why isn't PSHE on everyone's timetable?

The campaign to make PSHE statutory (and so subject to the same professional training, curriculum time and standards of rigour as other subjects) has the support of the Children's Commissioner, the Chief Medical Officer, the Association for Directors of Public Health, the Association of Police and Crime Commissioners, the Association of Independent Local Safeguarding Children Boards Chairs, two royal societies, five leading unions, six medical royal colleges, over 100 expert bodies and national organisations ranging from the NSPCC to The Samaritans, Relate and Teenage Cancer Trust, through to magazines such as *Cosmopolitan* and *Psychologies* (read more from *Psychologies* editor on pp.143–144). Some 85 per cent of business leaders, 88 per cent of teachers, 91 per cent of parents and 92 per cent of young people support change. And at the time of writing yet another Parliamentary Select Committee had reported on the unacceptable levels of PSHE in many of Britain's schools (around four in ten), arguing that poor performance would not be tolerated in other subjects and that there is a clear mismatch between the messages coming from government – on the importance of emotional wellbeing and character education in schools – compared with the practical steps taken to make them fundamental drivers in children's learning. Meanwhile, leading safety experts were pointing to reports confirming the number of children sexually exploited in Rotherham and calling again for the subject that educates children on issues such as sexual exploitation and abuse to become compulsory in schools.

'Schools are under a lot of pressure to deliver the curriculum, to see all children leave school reading and writing, and of course we support that,' says Joe Hayman, the PSHE Association chief executive who has been responsible for growing the campaign. 'We don't want it competing with those subjects, but it needs a place and it needs to be taught by trained teachers if it's going to deliver the benefits it can to children's wellbeing and their academic achievement.' Hayman points to research demonstrating that when taught well PSHE can create a positive cycle – with depression and anxiety levels reduced, and attendance and attainment going up. The PSHE Association also cites evidence that pupils who receive the lessons are more likely to have consenting relationships, use contraception when they have sex, and report abuse. They're also less likely to smoke, more likely to eat healthily and exercise more. The list goes on...

Hayman – like every supporter of the PSHE Association's campaign – believes that equipping children with the knowledge and skills they need as they face difficulties or form relationships is always going to be more effective and efficient than interventions later, when young people are demonstrating symptoms of mental health problems and struggling to get support when things have gone wrong. Perhaps in response to suggestions (often cited in defence of *non*-statutory status) that different areas of the country have different needs from the subject, the PSHE Association is also clear that no catchment or academic set is immune from family breakdown or family illness, trauma or loss (which can, of course, all impact on mental health); that all children need to understand different backgrounds, cultures and social groups and their role in tackling prejudice and discrimination in school or work, and that children and young people from all walks of life can, as a result of social media and the internet, learn all the wrong sorts of things about relationships in a way that can sabotage their own. The Association knows the PSHE lesson not only gives children and young people facts about life issues and windows into a world they need to understand if they're to enjoy and be successful in it, but crucially an expert, adult rather than fellow teen, perspective on them.

Can a 50-minute session deliver all that? 'PSHE lessons are only one piece of the puzzle,' says Hayman. 'It has to impact on the whole school and its ethos. If you promote a healthy, supportive culture in PSHE and staff don't model it in other classes, or support those ideas in the playground (for example, in the way students are encouraged to listen to, include and collaborate with each other) then it immediately undermines what's been done in the PSHE lesson. Students start to see it as something that is "nice but unrealistic". We want issues specifically explored in PSHE to be reinforced in other lessons, in other parts of the curriculum, and mirrored in behaviour policy.'

Hayman believes each school needs a clear subject lead like Di Harrill who has an equal place with other heads of departments and a voice at governors' meetings. This would give that teacher the opportunity to help other staff understand what's on the curriculum and how they can support it in their own work with the children. In addition, and crucially, the PSHE Association wants to see that precious regular slot on the timetable, so schools can slowly and appropriately build up knowledge of issues as children grow. One school, highlighted in the recent Parliamentary Select Committee report, had only delivered one PSHE lesson on sex and relationships in their primary school, and that was in the last term before children went into secondary school, long after many pupils might have started going through puberty or even seen and read about sex and relationships online or on TV.

But teachers need to be taught too and Hayman's view is that every single teacher should benefit from training in mental health and child development, and supported by proper professional development routes.

'One of the biggest barriers schools face is a lack of confidence among teachers who find issues like sex and relationships or eating disorders risky, believing that discussing them is likely to encourage rather than prevent behaviours,' says Joe. 'I understand why people are worried – these are complicated issues and often close to children's realities. Furthermore, in a class of 30, three or four may be experiencing some kind of mental health challenge.'

Hayman and his team at the PSHE Association have seen how training can put those teachers back in their comfort zone, giving them guidance about how to distance the learning from the learner (no personal experiences are discussed in class). It helps them put the subjects in proper context and gives them an understanding of how they can be discussed in a way that's acceptable and safe. The PSHE Association's resources map out how and why subjects can be developed at each key stage throughout the years (rather than being introduced at Key Stage 4 when issues are coming to a head).

For example, when looking at relationships (just one small part of the curriculum) at Key Stage 1 their programme of study would look at things such as good and bad feelings and simple strategies for managing them and communicating them to others. Things such as recognising what's fair, unfair, kind and unkind, right and wrong. Meanwhile, children at Key Stage 3 would be working on issues such as the features of positive stable relationships and those of unhealthy relationships; also looking at the fact that the media portrayal of relationships may not reflect real life. They would then look at bullying and abuse in all its forms, ways to challenge it, and support they can turn to. In the Key Stage 4 programme these relationship issues would include ways to manage changes in relationship and give pupils an awareness of exploitation, bullying and harassment and the unacceptability of physical, emotional or sexual abuse in all types of teenage relationships.

'Schools are incredibly busy, and under immense pressure, and I have nothing but admiration for head teachers who are pulling everything together,' says Hayman. 'But this stuff matters more than ever. What we want to help them see is that they have to start somewhere, and that PSHE is a good place to start and can help shape what their school does next.'

The PSHE Association is a registered charity and a membership organisation for education professionals. It can provide support, training and resources. If you'd like to find out more about its campaign to make PSHE statutory or sign up to benefit from its support, visit www.pshe-association.org.uk.

Index